Those who love cooking and baking tend to follow recipes in order to create a scrumptious dish or two. But what if the final dish was left up to chance? Or better yet, left up to you? A kind of adventure, where you meet the ingredients along the way and get an exciting recipe at the end?

Like the sound of that?
Well, that's exactly why you're here.

Flour had a plan – a plan to make a dish so wonderful and amazing – but he needed some help. He needed to find his friends. And his friends' friends. As how can Flour become a great dish without them?

Recipes need ingredients, and the recipe that Flour will be a part of is completely down to you. Who will you pick to be in Flour's team? Learn about each ingredient along the way and follow your choices to find out what recipe Flour and his friends become. Once you find the recipe, you can create and enjoy the dish!

This is an interactive book, which means that you don't read it in the same way as other books. Start with your first ingredient and follow the page numbers of your choice. There are many recipes to discover as you play this game, but if you're just searching for a delicious treat there's a recipe index at the back of the book.

This is a culinary adventure like no other. And remember, if you're a child reading this, find a grown-up to help you . . .
and if you're a grown-up, find a child to help you – it's always a case of the more the merrier when reading and cooking (and eating!) are involved.

Start on page 3 with your first ingredient, Flour.

Flour

People all over the world use some kind of flour – a fine powder made by grinding grains, nuts, seeds or roots. There's wheat flour, rice flour, cornflour, tapioca flour . . . hmm, what others can you think of? Some flours, such as wheat flour, contain a protein called gluten. Strong white bread flour has more gluten than plain flour, and water makes the gluten swell up to stretch when kneaded. Next time you add water to flour and knead it, see how elastic it becomes when you pull the two ends of the dough apart.

ALL PURPOSE flour

You must've met our dear friend Flour,
Who can turn into all kinds of food.
Like pasta, bread and biscuits,
Depending on our mood.

But now Flour doesn't know what to do.
And asks, 'What do you want to eat?'
A recipe needs some of Flour's friends . . .
Do you choose: **savoury or sweet?**

3

Sweet: go to page 4 (top shelf)
Savoury: go to page 8 (bottom shelf)

Sugar

Sweet: You chose Sugar!
So Flour asked if she was free.
Sugar did so love adventures,
Like a great new recipe.

Oh, Flour was so delighted,
And Sugar almost dropped her lid.
Now to find an 'oily' friend,
Will you choose: **solid** or **liquid**?

The sugar that we add to our cakes and hot drinks is extracted from sugar cane and sugar beet plants, and is called sucrose. Sucrose is made up of glucose and fructose molecules joined together.

It's worth remembering that sometimes a sweet recipe needs salt, and sometimes a savoury recipe needs sugar . . . everything needs balance to taste good. So even if you've chosen sugar now, your final recipe might need a pinch of salt, too.

Liquid: go to page 5 (top shelf)
Solid: go to page 4 (bottom shelf)

Margarine

Solid! You chose Margarine,
Otherwise known as Spread.
She often came second to Butter,
But is also good on bread.

Now Margarine began to wonder,
As making decisions was scary.
Each of us has different tastes,
Do you want: **spicy** or **dairy**?

In 1869, Napoleon III, the Emperor of France, set a challenge to find someone who could produce a butter substitute for the army and the poor. Hippolyte Mège-Mouriès was a French chemist who created margarine from beef fat and skimmed milk. Hands up if you'd like to try that? Today, margarine is made with vegetable oils and water. Phew!

Spicy: go to page 6 (top shelf)
Dairy: go to page 5 (bottom shelf)

Oil

Liquid! You chose Oil, you did,
But he's confused about what's new.
He was sleeping in the cupboard,
When asked to join the crew.

And the trouble with old, grouchy Oil
Was he didn't mix with all.
Do you choose one who is **fizzy**,
Or who lets Oil **float**, not fall?

Most oils are liquid at room temperature, and there are many different types used in cooking, made from plants and their seeds. These include sunflower oil, coconut oil (which is solid at room temperature) and rapeseed (or canola) oil. Have you seen those huge yellow fields of rapeseed flowers in the countryside? The seeds from those plants are harvested, heated and squeezed to get rapeseed oil.

Fizzy: go to page 8 (top shelf)
Float: go to page 6 (bottom shelf)

Milk

Dairy: You chose Milk!
And Milk was overjoyed.
Usually people spilled her,
And then she cried and cried.

Now Milk had a bit of a dilemma,
A healthy choice or cheeky sweets?
Well, everything in moderation,
Will you choose: **fruit** or **cocoa** treats?

The phrase 'there's no point crying over spilt milk', meaning there's no point getting upset over something that's already happened, came about through folk tales about fairies. Apparently, fairies love milk, so if any is spilt you need not worry as the fairies will come and drink it all up.

Cocoa: go to page 7 (top shelf)
Fruit: go to page 7 (bottom shelf)

Ginger

Spicy: You chose Ginger!
Though not a spice as such,
She adds some heat to dishes,
When chillies are too much.

Ginger knew just what to do,
She thought of who would suit.
The friend to choose should be quite sweet,
But: a **golden liquid** or **crunchy fruit**?

Ginger contains the chemicals gingerol, zingerone and shogaol, which give it its 'spiciness'! Gingerol is very similar to capsaicin, which is what makes chillies hot.

It's really useful to eat a piece of ginger if you have motion sickness when travelling. Ginger can soothe the stomach and keep your blood pressure steady.

Crunchy fruit: go to page 9 (top shelf)
Golden liquid: go to page 9 (bottom shelf)

Oil floats: You chose Water!
And Water said, 'Eau yay!'
Flour said, 'We need one more,
Who can we choose today?'

Water thought about his friends,
Which flavours did he know?
His **barky friend** or **bean pod mate**,
The two he helped to grow.

Water

Water is so important for life on Earth: without it we wouldn't exist. Every single cell in our body needs water – it helps to maintain our body temperature, remove waste (yes, wee and poo!) and get all the good stuff, or nutrients, from our food around to all our organs via the blood.

Oil is less dense than water, so when poured onto water, the oil floats. Try it and see!

6

Bean pod: go to page 11 (top shelf)
Barky: go to page 11 (bottom shelf)

Chocolate Chips

Good choice, the treat, the Chocolate Chips!
You have everything for a bake.
It'll be melty, chocolatey and yummy,
Though not quite a biscuit or cake.

Have you ever tried eating cooking chocolate? There's a difference between the chocolate chips you use for baking and the chocolate bars you eat straight from the wrapper. Baking chocolate often has less sugar in it, so it's quite bitter and snaps easily. Eating chocolate has added sugar and milk, so it's very soft and sweet.

Now you have all your ingredients, turn to page 23 to find out what dish they could turn into.

Good choice, the fruit, the Raisins!
You now have your ingredient team.
Time to try out the recipe . . .
It'll need some jam and cream!

Raisins

Raisins are dried grapes. The process by which this happens was discovered accidentally, probably around 2000 BC, when grapes were left in the sun and shrivelled up. Different grapes and drying processes give us different coloured raisins, and even sultanas! Unfortunately, you can't turn a raisin back into a grape by adding water, but they do plump up a bit when cooked.

7

Now you have all your ingredients, turn to page 22 to find out what dish they could turn into.

Baking Powder

Both baking powder and bicarbonate of soda are raising agents – that is, they make cakes and breads rise . . . but there is a difference. Acids and alkalis react to make carbon dioxide bubbles, which causes bread dough and cake batter to rise. Bicarbonate of soda is an alkali, so needs an acid (such as lemon juice) to work. Baking powder is both acid and alkali, so starts fizzing as soon as it is added to anything wet. Add some to water and see what happens!

Fizzy: You chose Baking Powder!
Who reacts well with anyone.
A really supportive, bubbly friend,
Raising the spirits of everyone.

Of course he likes cool recipes,
Trying anything incredible.
But who would be the best to choose . . .
A **curd** or maybe a **vegetable**?

Vegetable: go to page 13 (top shelf)
Curd: go to page 13 (bottom shelf)

Savoury: You chose Salt!
The saltiest rock on the list.
He likes to turn up everywhere,
And doesn't want to be missed.

Yes, Salt is really salty,
But dissolved he tastes more bold.
How much he would dissolve though,
Depended on how **warm** or **cold**.

Salt

Salt (sodium chloride) is important for our cells and organs to work correctly. We actually crave salt when our body needs it. Because salt is so important, it has always been valuable. Salt was used as a payment for Roman soldiers, which is how we got the word 'salary', from the Latin word '*sal*', meaning 'salt'.

It's worth remembering that sometimes a savoury recipe needs sugar, and sometimes a sweet recipe needs salt . . . everything needs balance to taste good. So even if you've chosen salt now, your final recipe might need a pinch of sugar, too.

Cold: go to page 10 (top shelf)
Warm: go to page 12 (bottom shelf)

Apple

Good choice, the fruit, the Apple!
Now to create a delicious pudding.
Pair it with ice cream or custard . . .
Or maybe cream's the perfect thing?

FUJI

HONEY CRISP

GRANNY SMITH

FRESH

LA

LU'S BEST

Golden Delicious

If you're an apple grower, you're interested in the science of pomology, which is easy to remember if you know the French word for apple: 'la pomme'. Apples are members of the rose family, which is why apple blossoms look like teeny roses. Pears, peaches, plums and cherries belong to the rose family, too.

Now you have all your ingredients, turn to page 24 to find out what dish they could turn into.

Golden Syrup

Good choice, the liquid, Golden Syrup!
Because of sugar he is the sweetest.
Ideal when baking biscuits,
Which are neater than the neatest!

454 g

Created in London in the 1880s, golden syrup isn't actually liquid gold, but a golden-coloured, see-through liquid. It's an inverted syrup, in which the sugars are broken down, making it taste so much sweeter.

Golden syrup can be used instead of runny honey in recipes. Both golden syrup and honey are thicker and more dense than water, so if you pour water on top of syrup or honey, you'll find the water just sits there without mixing. Try it and see!

9

Now you have all your ingredients, turn to page 25 to find out what dish they could turn into.

Cold Water

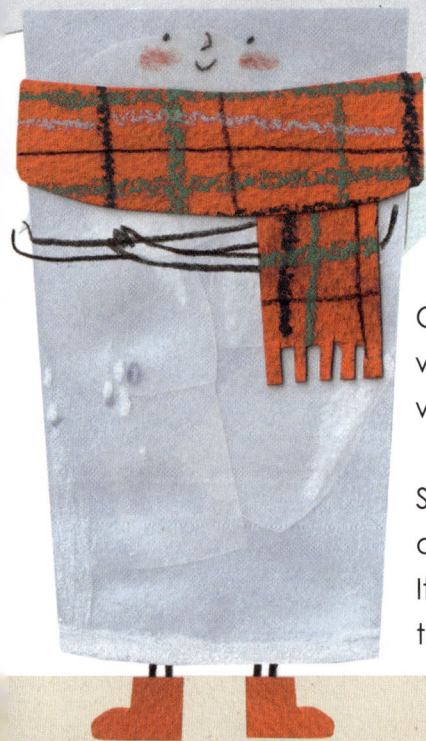

Cold: You chose Cold Water!
He could be icy or straight from the tap.
And much better than a cup of coffee,
To wake someone up from a nap.

Cold Water was so excited,
As if it's a game he could win.
He could think of his friend **super tuber**,
Or his bestie who **lives in a tin**.

Cold water is useful for flaky pastries, when you don't want the fat to melt while you're making it.

Sprinkling cold water on someone who is asleep will most definitely wake them up. It is a shock (so be careful who you try this out on), causing the body to release the fight-or-flight hormone, adrenaline, which it does whenever we're scared, excited or stressed. Adrenaline makes the heart beat faster, sending more blood to the brain and muscles, so we can react quicker . . . and either shout (fight) or jump up and run (flight)!

Lives in a tin: go to page 12 (top shelf)
Super tuber: go to page 10 (bottom shelf)

Potato

Super tuber: You chose Potato!
Who is such a starchy kind.
He's happily boiled, chipped or mashed,
He honestly doesn't mind.

He had two friends he really liked,
They were the best of mates.
But do you pick the **melty block**
Or a **vine with punchy traits**?

Potatoes are part of a family of flowering plants known as Solanaceae, which includes tomatoes and aubergines. Deadly nightshade (*Atropa belladonna*), known simply as belladonna, is from the same family, which is why Solanaceae are known as the 'nightshades'. Great name for a rock band, huh?

Punchy vine: go to page 15 (top shelf)
Melty block: go to page 15 (bottom shelf)

Vanilla

Good choice, bean pod mate, Vanilla!
This extract was in no way a fake.
Such a *well-loved* and comforting flavour,
To add to a teeny, tiny cake.

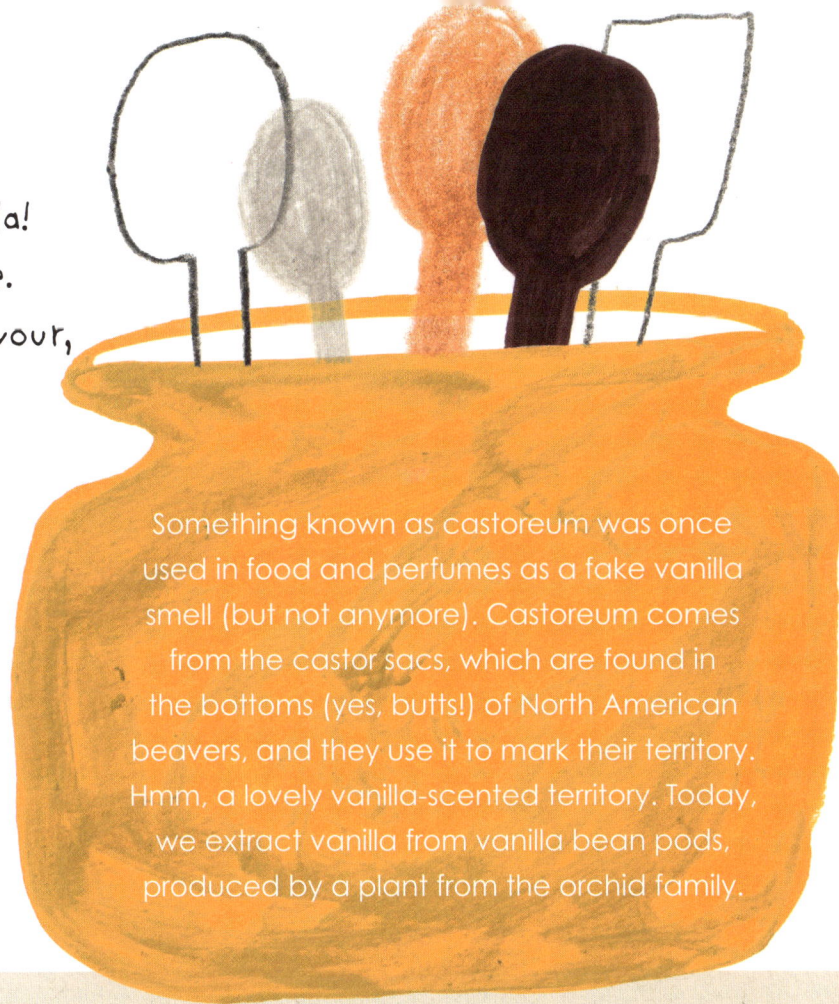

Something known as castoreum was once used in food and perfumes as a fake vanilla smell (but not anymore). Castoreum comes from the castor sacs, which are found in the bottoms (yes, butts!) of North American beavers, and they use it to mark their territory. Hmm, a lovely vanilla-scented territory. Today, we extract vanilla from vanilla bean pods, produced by a plant from the orchid family.

Now you have all your ingredients, turn to page 27 to find out what dish they could turn into.

cinnamon

Good choice, the barky friend it is!
Old Cinnamon is the final one,
Who can flavour almost anything,
Not just that Scandi bun.

Cinnamon is a spice created from the inner bark of cinnamon trees, first discovered in Sri Lanka. It is used in many dishes around the world, but is most popular as a flavouring in the famous Scandinavian bun or roll. This cinnamon bun is known as kanelbulle in Sweden, kanelsnegl in Denmark, and kanelbolle and kanelsnurr in Norway. 'Kanel' means cinnamon.

Now you have all your ingredients, turn to page 26 to find out what dish they could turn into.

Lives in a tin: You chose Ghee!
She was ready for what came next
As making quick decisions
Never left her feeling vexed.

There's always time for recipes,
And Ghee got ready today.
But are the **leftovers from the fridge**
Or **'fresh' from a can** right away?

Ghee

Ghee is clarified, unsalted butter, which means butter has been melted and simmered to remove the water and milk solids. It is popular in South Asian cooking, as well as being used as the fuel for small clay lamps lit during Diwali or Deepavali, the festival of lights celebrated by Hindus, Sikhs and Jains all over the world. Deepavali, meaning 'a path or row of lamps', marks the New Year: new beginnings, celebratory food and togetherness. Some remember the story of Lord Rama defeating the demon king Ravana, while others think of Lord Krishna defeating the demon Narakasura. Either way it is a celebration of overcoming darkness (evil, ignorance, sadness) with light (good, wisdom, happiness).

Leftovers: go to page 16 (top shelf)
Can: go to page 16 (bottom shelf)

Warm: You chose Warm Water!
She was as warm as one can be.
And could float above Cold Water,
An amazing trick to see.

'Oh yes, I know,' she warmly said,
'They're perfect, and so cute.
You can choose a great **fun guy**,
Or an **oil squeezed from a fruit**.'

Warm Water

Warm water is useful in cooking when we want something to dissolve. For example, if we took a solid like salt and mixed it in a liquid like water, it would dissolve faster in warm water than in cold. Try adding a bit of food colouring to some warm water and pouring it over some cold water. You'll see the coloured warm water stays on top, because warm water, like warm air, rises or floats. Eventually it'll all mix together, though.

Oil: go to page 14 (top shelf)
Fun guy: go to page 14 (bottom shelf)

Carrot

Before the sixteenth century, carrots were purple. When some random yellow and orange ones popped up, Dutch farmers decided to keep growing these in order to make orange carrots popular: the national colour of the Netherlands is orange, in honour of Prince Willem van Oranje-Nassau, who was responsible for Dutch independence.

Carrots are one of the sweetest vegetables around, which is why they're actually bad for rabbits' teeth!

Good choice, the vegetable, sweet Carrot!
Originally purple, such a tease.
A natural plant-based sweetener,
Used in bakes topped with cream cheese.

Now you have all your ingredients, turn to page 28 to find out what dish they could turn into.

Yoghurt

Good choice, the curd, it's Yoghurt!
He's ever so creamy and white.
Use him to make a smooth batter,
And deep-fry for the swirliest bite.

In the Middle East and Asia, where it's really hot, it's quite cooling to drink yoghurt drinks. The Indian lassi is a runny yoghurt drink, often mixed with squished fruit such as mango. Greek yoghurt is famous for its thick creaminess, and it gets this texture when the extra liquid is drained out by leaving it hanging in some cloth.

Now you have all your ingredients, turn to page 30 to find out what dish they could turn into.

Olive Oil

Oil from a fruit: You chose Olive Oil!
A fabulous, popular sort.
Remember that olives are fruits,
Not veggies as many first thought.

Olive Oil was rich and expensive,
Fine dining had put her on the map.
Her best friends were famous in phrases,
After 'Open . . .', or when **taking a snap.**

Olives are fruits, and their oil is one of the most expensive oils in the world, especially when the olives are handpicked. A paste is made by grinding down the olives and then pressing the paste to extract, or squeeze out, as much of the oil as possible. Next time you're at the supermarket, have a look at the different colours of olive oil. This is all down to the type of olive used, how it was pressed, and the climate during harvesting.

Snap: go to page 17 (top shelf)
Open: go to page 17 (bottom shelf)

Yeast

Fun guy: You chose Yeast!
Who bakers love and adore.
And biologists like to study,
To learn a little bit more.

This teeny, tiny organism,
Loves to be used in bread baking.
Joined by **light bulbs** or a **powdery pal,**
Which one will you be making?

Yeast is a type of fungus (the plural is fungi . . . 'fun guy'!), and it's a single-celled living organism (yes, an ingredient that's alive!). It is present all around us in the air, soil and on plants. There are so many different kinds of yeast, and one of the most ancient types of leavened (raised) bread used natural yeast from the air to make the dough rise. We make sourdough bread this way even today.

Light bulbs: go to page 18 (top shelf)
Powdery pal: go to page 18 (bottom shelf)

Black Pepper

Good choice, punchy vine, it's Black Pepper!
They leave our tongues a-tingling.
Been paired with salt for many years,
And ideal for a teeny dumpling.

Piper nigrum, or black pepper, originally from southern India, is now used all over the world to add flavour to meals. The peppercorns are dried berries, and these berries grow on a flowering vine, a bit like grapes.

No one actually knows when salt and pepper became a pair, but it's thought that in the seventeenth century, King Louis XIV of France made black pepper popular. He wasn't keen on seasoning his food, but felt pepper added just enough of a punch without overpowering his meal.

Now you have all your ingredients, turn to page 32 to find out what dish they could turn into.

Melted Butter

Good choice, the block, Melted Butter!
Looks like oil when poured in a glass.
Much yellower – from the milk of a cow
Who has eaten the lushest green grass.

Butter is made by the churning of cream or milk. As cream has a higher amount of fat than milk, you can easily make your own butter by shaking a small amount of double cream in a jar (make sure the lid is on firmly!). Shaking brings all the fat in the cream together to form a solid lump of yellow butter. The leftover white liquid is buttermilk.

Now you have all your ingredients, turn to page 33 to find out what dish they could turn into.

Leftover Curry

Good choice, it's Leftover Curry!
Let's not throw a morsel away.
Wrapped into triangle parcels,
We'll have a new dish for today.

Although we're talking about leftover curry here, you could use anything that's a leftover: the last bit of cheese in the fridge, pieces of fruit, last night's pasta . . . all that matters is that we're not throwing anything away. In the UK we throw away almost 7 million tonnes of food every year – that's nearly the same weight as 400,000 double decker buses. And when one in ten people around the world are actually starving, that's difficult to swallow.

Now you have all your ingredients, turn to page 34 to find out what dish they could turn into.

Condensed Milk

Good choice, the can, Condensed Milk!
'Oh Wow,' the Condensed Milk said,
'I never thought that I could be used . . .
. . . in a recipe for a savoury bread.'

Condensed milk was invented in the 1800s as a way to store milk – it can keep for years in a can! It is cow's milk with about two-thirds of the water removed, and sometimes has added sugar as well. Condensed milk has a very thick, creamy, syrup-like look when poured from the can, and is used to make many different sweets and desserts, such as coconut ice and fudge. When a can is very gently heated, the milk becomes dulce de leche, a sweet caramel sauce.

since 1947
condensed milk
sweet

16

Now you have all your ingredients, turn to page 37 to find out what dish they could turn into.

Cheese

Good choice, taking a snap — it's Cheese,
We shout out his name so we smile.
Now, a Mexican dish, so easily made,
And perfect when stacked in a pile.

It's thought that over 8,000 years ago, milk was left out in the sun and bacteria in the air caused it to curdle or become lumpy. And those lumpy curds were cheese! This isn't safe to do today; instead we add acid (such as lemon juice) to warm milk to create the same effect. When we take photos, we ask people to 'say cheese'. By saying the 'ee' sound they show off their teeth and look like they're grinning.

Now you have all your ingredients, turn to page 39 to find out what dish they could turn into.

Sesame Seeds

Good choice, after 'Open' . . . it's Sesame!
From 'Ali Baba and the Forty Thieves'.
We squeeze oil from the nutritious seeds,
And eat their fennel-flavoured leaves.

SESAME SEEDS

The *Sesamum indicum* plant is found in Africa and Asia, and its seeds were one of the first to be used to make oil, as far back as 3000 BC. Sesame oil is very popular in cooking and has many medicinal uses too. In the story of 'Ali Baba and the Forty Thieves', the magical phrase 'Open Sesame' was the code to open the cave where the thieves had hidden their treasure.

Kitchen Creations   Nigel Lawson →
Speedy Sauces
DELISH RECIPES   Lucia Vinti

Now you have all your ingredients, turn to page 38 to find out what dish they could turn into.

Garlic Butter

Good choice, light bulbs, it's Garlic Butter,
Who flavours all dishes with ease.
Especially starters of Italian bread,
Why not add a sprinkling of cheese?

In folklore, it is said that garlic bulbs keep vampires and other scary spirits away. But why? Well, garlic is stinky and also antibacterial thanks to its sulfur-based chemicals, and so keeps people healthy. 'Vampires' might've simply been those suffering from a deadly disease. The healthy garlic-eaters believed that garlic kept ill people and their diseases away.

Now you have all your ingredients, turn to page 40 to find out what dish they could turn into.

Powdered Milk

Good choice, so powdery is Powdered Milk
And always so handy to store.
'Not only for milk,' said our powdery friend,
'I can be added and turned into more.'

Powdered milk, invented by the Russian doctor Osip Krichevsky in 1802, is made by evaporating the water in milk until it's dry and powdery. Powdered milk can be stored better and for longer in airtight containers, as it's so dry that no nasty bacteria or mould can grow in it and cause it to spoil or go off. You also don't need to keep it in the fridge. It's useful to add to recipes when you only need a small amount of milk. Saves having to open a whole 'proper' bottle!

Now you have all your ingredients, turn to page 42 to find out what dish they could turn into.

Useful Tips

Now, before the next part of the adventure . . . SAFETY! All these recipes involve a kind of heat, whether it's an oven, hob, frying in hot oil, making sugar syrup, or pouring boiling water from a kettle. Always ask an adult for help and be really careful.

When deep-frying, dip a wooden spoon into the oil – if bubbles start to appear gently and steadily around the spoon, then you're ready to fry!

Once a frying pan is hot, it'll cook the next batches of whatever you're making quicker than the first. So sometimes it's useful to reduce the heat.

Use utensils such as spatulas to flip flatbreads and pancakes over in hot frying pans. If you're using a dry pan to cook flatbreads, dust off any extra flour from the bread, as often the flour stays in the pan and burns, which can stick to the next flatbread making it taste a little burnt, too.

The best type of frying pan is a large (24cm diameter), heavy-based, non-stick one. Make sure you have everything rolled out and ready before the pan is hot. When deep-frying, a deeper pan is useful, and smaller pans need less oil.

Wear oven gloves when using a hot oven, and make sure all surfaces are protected from hot baking trays. Remember not to eat anything straight out of the oven – always leave your bakes to cool first . . . although warm, squishy cookies are okay, as they're rather lush. Using the fan setting on your oven means they cook faster. The temperature is lower on this setting and saves energy.

All ovens are different, so baking times may vary. The bakes in this book used the middle shelf of the oven. It's best not to keep opening the oven to check if your bakes are ready, as this can cause the oven temperature to cool and cause cakes to sink in the middle.

When using knives and graters, food processors or blenders make sure your fingers aren't too near the sharp blades.

Make sure you wash your hands before and after handling food (no one wants to eat scones made by hands that have just petted a dog!). And always clean cooking surfaces and utensils after use, especially when working with uncooked and cooked foods, which shouldn't mix.

The recipes in this book are written in the same way as 'regular' cookbooks, so you may need to know a few things before you start. There are handy definitions and explanations in the Glossary on pages 70–74.

Even though you discovered your ingredient friends in a certain order, ingredients are listed in recipes in the order we use them – they're all still there, though!

Flour and sugar have many forms, so examples are given for which is best for each recipe. Self-raising flour already contains raising agents, so we can make fluffier scones and cakes. Sometimes cake batters are heavy, like when carrots are added, so you may need self-raising flour and a raising agent. You may also want to experiment with gluten-free flours, different sugars (finer sugars for sprinkling, large-grained sugars for a lovely crunch, and brown sugars for a golden colour), and dairy-free alternatives (such as vegan spreads, cheeses and plant-based milks). Butter, margarine, ghee and oil can be swapped for each other for slightly different results, but remember that some fats contain salt already, so taste things before you add salt! Even different varieties of potatoes give different results. Why not bake a dish instead of frying it? Ideas are given in each recipe.

If you ever find that a dough is too sticky, add a little flour. If it's too dry, add a little water. Some flours need less water than others, so add water gradually. (There are several recipes in this book where Water makes a guest appearance to help his team go with the flow! Can you find them?)

When baking with yeast, keep salt away from the yeast at the start. Salt adds flavour but stops the yeast from growing, which is a problem if it hasn't yet grown enough. We also don't want the yeast to get too bubbly, so salt is important in bread-making to control yeast growth for an even bread texture. Warm water (not hot) and sugar also help yeast grow.

There are maths tricks too. If you need to make more than, say, 12 cookies, you're welcome to double up the ingredient amounts and make 24 – the recipes in this book work well multiplied up or divided down. For liquid measurements, 1 teaspoon is 5ml and 1 tablespoon is 15ml, so how many tablespoons make 60ml? By adding 1 teaspoon of baking powder for every 100g of plain flour, you can make your own self-raising flour. And if you need to split dough into equal balls, you can weigh the whole piece and divide it by the number of balls you need. That way, each portion is the same weight. Having a good set of weighing scales helps!

And finally . . . The recipes here are simplified versions of traditional recipes, so won't be exactly how our parents, grandparents or professional chefs make them, but the dishes will still be utterly delicious. Recipes are just guidelines – you can add more ingredients and experiment! In this book we use 47 ingredients (and a few surprise guests, too), so why not see what unique recipes you come up with? Spices, herbs and seasonings make dishes exciting, so choose ones you like. Remember, cooking is about practice and experience: the more you do it, the more you'll understand the science of how ingredients behave and what works well together. Then you can predict what will happen, and know that your dish will taste delicious.

Go on, have a try. Invent your recipes now!
The adventures really never stop.

Fruit Scones

A scone is a type of bread, usually eaten as a teatime treat. Scones can be made plain or with added fruit, such as raisins. They're thought to have originated from Scotland, and yet the biggest arguments are further south, about whether to say 'sk-on' or 'sk-own'. And of course the debate between Cornwall (putting jam on your scone first, then cream) and Devon (putting cream on your scone, then jam). We'd like to think you need to make the scone first before any topping gets a look in.

Have a quick read of pages 19–21 before you try out this recipe.

6–8 large scones

45 minutes

350g self-raising flour, and a little extra for dusting

85g caster sugar

85g cold margarine (or butter)

75g raisins

175ml milk

1. Preheat the oven to 220°C (190°C fan). Line a baking tray.
2. Sift the flour into a bowl and add the sugar.
3. Add the margarine and rub it into the flour-sugar mixture with your fingers until it looks like breadcrumbs.
4. Mix in the raisins. You can still use your hands.
5. Add about 150ml of the milk and knead to make a firm but crumbly dough. Don't overwork or knead it too much, and add a little more milk if it's still too dry.
6. Bring the dough together on a floured board or surface (use as little flour as possible) and flatten the dough to the thickness of your scone cutter, or to about 3–4cm thick.
7. Cut out your scone dough rounds (using a 7cm cutter) and add them to the baking tray.
8. Bring together the leftover scraps of dough gently (without kneading too much) and cut more rounds, repeating until all the dough is used up.
9. Brush the scone rounds with the leftover milk using a pastry brush (making sure not to drip milk down the sides of the scones), and bake them in the oven for 20–25 minutes, until golden brown on top.
10. Take the scones out of the oven, leave to cool on a wire rack and then enjoy with jam and cream!

Jam

Now turn to page 68 or . . .
Let's go meet a nutty sweet (page 44)
and find out what's in store!

Chocolate Chip Cookies

Cookies are bigger and softer in texture than biscuits, and these have little bits of chocolate in them that are soft and melty when straight out of the oven. There's a story that an American chef called Ruth Wakefield tried to make a chocolate cookie dough in the 1930s, but the chocolate she added didn't melt fully, which meant there were tiny chunks of chocolate throughout. These were the first ever chocolate chip cookies, also known as Toll House cookies.

Have a quick read of pages 19–21 before you try out this recipe.

25–30 cookies
45 minutes

225g caster sugar
225g margarine (or softened butter), and a little extra for greasing
4 tablespoons (60ml) milk (or 2 tablespoons (30ml) condensed milk)
170g chocolate chips
340g self-raising flour
1 teaspoon vanilla extract (optional)

1. Preheat the oven to 180°C (160°C fan). Grease and line two baking trays.
2. Cream the sugar and margarine together in a bowl using a fork.
3. Add the milk and chocolate chips. (Use condensed milk instead of regular milk for chewier cookies, and add the vanilla extract too at this stage for extra flavour, if you'd like.)
4. Add the flour and mix well until you have a dough.
5. Use your hands to roll 25–30 walnut-sized cookie dough balls, about 30–40g each. If you don't want to bake all the cookies right away, the dough balls can be kept in the freezer for up to 3 months.
6. Place the dough balls onto the baking trays.
7. Flatten each ball with a fork. Leave some space between each one as they will spread during baking. (Freezing the biscuits before baking makes them spread less, as the fat becomes solid in the freezer, so doesn't melt and spread as quickly when baked.)
7. Bake the cookies for 25–30 minutes, until golden brown.
8. Leave the cookies to cool a little on a wire rack and enjoy while still warm!

Now turn to page 68 or . . .
Introduce the softest silk (page 46) and find out what's in store!

Ginger and Apple Crumble

Because of rationing during World War Two, pie pastry couldn't always be made, and so the crumble was invented. This meant that the limited ingredients could go further . . . you didn't need a lot of fat and flour to make a lovely crumble.

   Crumbles aren't always sweet and fruity. You can make savoury ones too, with vegetables and salty, cheesy toppings, or using herbs and black pepper instead of sugar.

Have a quick read of pages 19–21 before you try out this recipe.

4–6 servings

1 hour

500g apples
150g plain or self-raising flour
75g Demerara sugar
1 teaspoon ground ginger
75g cold margarine (or butter)

1. Preheat the oven to 200°C (180°C fan).
2. Core and peel the apples and cut them into 1cm cubes. Place the apple cubes into a 20cm diameter cake tin or baking dish.
3. In a bowl, mix the flour, sugar and ginger together.
4. Rub the margarine into this flour mixture using your fingers until it looks like breadcrumbs.
5. Sprinkle these 'breadcrumbs' over the top of the apples and press down a little.
6. Bake for 35–40 minutes, until golden brown. Serve with custard, cream or ice cream.

Now turn to page 68 or . . .
There's someone who is sparkly (page 48), let's find out what's in store!

Fairings

Originally these biscuits were sold at fairs as edible souvenirs for people to buy for their sweethearts. But the ginger version, unique to Cornwall, is known as a Cornish fairing or ginger fairing. A crunchy, sweet and spicy biscuit to dunk in your tea.

Have a quick read of pages 19–21 before you try out this recipe.

1. Preheat the oven to 200°C (180°C fan). Line two baking trays.
2. In a bowl, mix the flour and ground ginger together. (Another ingredient you can add is chopped stem or crystallised ginger to make it more gingery, if you'd like!)
3. Heat the margarine, sugar and golden syrup in a pan over a medium heat for 2–3 minutes until melted.
4. Make a well in the bowl containing the flour and ginger, and pour in the sweet, melted margarine mix. Mix well until you have a dough.
5. Split the dough into 16 small balls, about 30g each. Flatten them with the back of a spoon so that each biscuit is about 1cm thick and 6cm in diameter.
6. Place them on the lined baking trays, spaced equally apart, and bake for 8–10 minutes, until golden brown.
7. Leave the fairings on the baking tray for 5 minutes, then leave to cool completely on a wire rack before eating.

16 biscuits
40 minutes

245g self-raising flour
1 tablespoon ground ginger
100g margarine (or butter)
90g Demerara sugar
4 tablespoons (60ml) golden syrup
1 tablespoon stem or crystallised ginger, finely chopped (optional)

Now turn to page 68 or . . .
There's someone oat-ally awesome (page 49), let's find out what's in store!

Churros

It isn't known who invented these sweet fried treats, but it's likely that they were created in Spain and then taken around the world by the Spanish and Portuguese. Churros are famous in Spain, Portugal and Mexico, sprinkled with sugar and dipped in hot chocolate sauce, or a drink known as champurrado.

Have a quick read of pages 19–21 before you try out this recipe.

15–18 small churro bites

45 minutes

165ml water
150g caster sugar
4 tablespoons (60ml) vegetable oil, and more for deep-frying
250g self-raising flour, sifted
2 teaspoons ground cinnamon
A pinch of salt (optional)
Chocolate sauce (optional)

1. Pour the water into a pan and bring it to the boil.
2. Add 30g of sugar to the water and stir until it's dissolved. Add the oil too. (You could also add a pinch of salt to balance the sweetness, if you'd like.)
3. Take the pan off the heat, add the sifted flour to the pan and mix well, making sure there are no lumps. Leave this dough to cool.
4. Mix the rest of the sugar and cinnamon in a bowl. Leave this to one side.
5. Fill a piping bag with the dough mix. (Usually a 2cm star-nozzle is attached to piping bags to make traditional churros.)
6. Line a plate with kitchen roll ready to receive the fried churros.
7. Pour some oil into a deep pan until the pan is about one-third full. Heat the oil on a medium heat until a small amount of batter floats to the surface and starts to fry when added to the oil (see page 19 for another tip).
8. You will need help for this next part. Pipe the dough directly over the hot oil, and ask someone to cut the piped dough every 5–6cm using scissors, so that small pieces (single churros) fall into the oil gently. You should be able to cook 5–6 churros at a time.
9. Fry the churros for 2–3 minutes until they expand and turn golden brown. Take them out of the oil using a slotted spoon and transfer to the plate lined with kitchen roll, to drain any excess oil.
10. While still warm, toss the drained churros in the bowl of cinnamon sugar until fully coated.
11. Cook the next batch of churros in the same way.
12. Enjoy the churros as they are, or dip them into chocolate sauce, if you'd like.

Now turn to page 68 or . . .
Check the calendar (page 50), invite a friend, and find out what's in store!

Vanilla Cupcakes

The idea of cakes baked in small cups was first described in 1796 by Amelia Simmons in a book called *American Cookery*. They were originally called 'number cakes' – it was another American food writer, Eliza Leslie, who called them cupcakes in 1828. This recipe is based on the Italian 'torta all'acqua', or 'water cake', which uses no dairy products.

Have a quick read of pages 19–21 before you try out this recipe.

18 cupcakes
40 minutes

225g caster sugar
4 tablespoons (60ml)
  vegetable oil
340ml water
1 teaspoon vanilla extract
340g self-raising flour
Icing sugar (optional)

1. Preheat the oven to 200°C (180°C fan). Line two cupcake trays with paper cupcake cases (enough for 18 cupcakes).
2. Whisk the sugar, oil, water and vanilla extract in a measuring jug, until the sugar has dissolved and the mixture is quite frothy.
3. Put the flour into a bowl, make a well in the middle and pour in the mixture from the measuring jug.
4. Beat everything well for 3–4 minutes to make sure it's all mixed and there are no lumps. It should be a smooth, runny batter.
5. Divide the mixture equally into the cupcake cases.
6. Bake for 15–20 minutes, until a dinner knife or toothpick comes out clean and dry when pushed into the middle of one of the cupcakes.
7. Leave to cool on a wire rack, then dust with icing sugar, if you'd like, and serve.

Now turn to page 68 or . . .
Just ask the bees (page 51) to help you,
and find out what's in store!

Carrot Cake

Originally, carrot cakes were baked in a pastry case, a bit like a pie. In the Middle East, carrot puddings, such as carrot halva, were (and still are!) very popular; it's thought that carrot cakes were invented because if carrot puddings used carrots as sweeteners instead of sugar, why couldn't we do the same with cake?

Have a quick read of pages 19–21 before you try out this recipe.

6–8 slices

1 hour

200g self-raising flour, sifted
60g sugar, such as dark brown soft or caster sugar
1 teaspoon baking powder
60g carrots, finely grated
3 tablespoons (45ml) sunflower or vegetable oil, and a little extra for greasing
150ml water
1 teaspoon mixed spice (optional)
Icing sugar (optional)

1. Preheat the oven to 200°C (180°C) fan. Grease and line a 900g/2lb (23 x 13 x 7cm) loaf tin.
2. In a bowl, mix the flour, sugar and baking powder together really well. Add the mixed spice too, if using. (If you're using dark brown soft sugar, make sure it mixes in well, without any lumps.)
3. Add the grated carrots and mix until each carrot piece is nicely coated in the floury mix.
4. Into another bowl or measuring jug, whisk together the oil and water. Pour this into the carrot mixture and fold together, mixing well.
5. Transfer this batter into the loaf tin and bake for 30–40 minutes, until a dinner knife or toothpick comes out clean and dry when pushed into the middle of the cake.
6. Once the cake has cooled, you can add a dusting of icing sugar if you'd like, or spread some cream cheese icing on top (see bonus recipe, page 29).

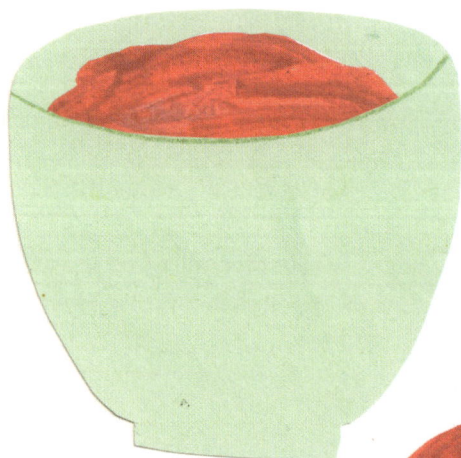

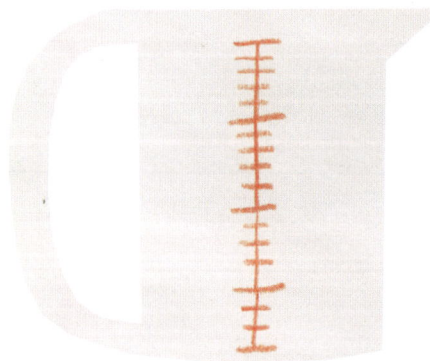

Now turn to page 68 or . . .
Call the influencer, instant gram (page 56), to find out what's in store!

Cinnamon Cream Cheese Icing

15 minutes

25g butter (or margarine), softened
125g cream cheese
50g icing sugar, sifted
½ teaspoon ground cinnamon
A few drops of vanilla extract
  (optional)

1. Whisk the butter, cream cheese and vanilla extract, if using, until mixed well.
2. Sift in the icing sugar and cinnamon a little at a time, whisking carefully until it is all smooth.
3. Spread over the cooled cake!

Tip

This cake isn't huge, as cakes baked with vegetables, fresh fruit, and with cream cheese icing, can spoil quickly. If you do have any cake left over, though, keep it in the fridge but enjoy at room temperature.

Jalebi

Also known as mushabak, jal-vallika and zalabia, jalebi (pronounced 'jeh-lay-bee') is a crispy, sugar-syrup-soaked treat presented in circular, squiggly shapes. It was mentioned for the first time as 'zulabiya' in Arabic, in a thirteenth-century cookbook by Muhammad bin Hasan al-Baghdadi.

Have a quick read of pages 19–21 before you try out this recipe.

40–45 jalebi
1 hour 30 minutes

145g plain flour
125ml plain yoghurt
425ml water
300g caster or Demerara sugar
¼ teaspoon baking powder
Vegetable oil, for deep-frying
3 cardamom pods, slightly cracked open
   (optional)
A pinch of saffron strands (optional)
A few drops of orange food colouring
   (optional)
1 tablespoon (15ml) lemon juice or a
   small (15g) wedge of lemon (optional)

1. Mix the flour and yoghurt in a bowl. It will look lumpy, so don't worry!

2. Slowly add 140ml of water to the bowl, whisking until it turns into a smooth batter that isn't too runny or too thick. This is known as a soft dropping consistency: when you lift up the whisk, the batter falls off in a slow stream. Leave this batter to one side for 15–20 minutes.

3. In a large pan over a medium heat, mix the sugar with 285ml of water until the sugar dissolves. As it starts to boil, you can add cardamom pods and/or saffron strands for extra flavour, as well as drops of orange food colouring, if you'd like. You could also add some lemon juice or a wedge of lemon for extra tangy flavour; it also helps to stop the sugar syrup crystallising.

4. Boil the syrup for 10–15 minutes until the syrup is thicker, but still runny, a bit like maple syrup. Leave the syrup to one side. It will thicken as it cools, but make sure it stays warm (it should be warm when you add the fried jalebis in step 8; if not, warm it up a little on the hob).

5. Whisk the baking powder into the batter and pour it into a piping bag or an old (but clean!) squeezy sauce bottle. The hole or nozzle should be about 5mm in diameter.

6. Pour oil into a deep pan until the pan is about one-third full. Heat the oil over a medium heat until a small amount of batter floats to the surface and starts to fry when added to the oil (see page 19 for another tip).

7. Pipe the batter in 5–6 circular 'doodles' directly into the hot oil, being very careful. Imagine you're doodling 6cm diameter spiral snail shells – or why not try doodling your name or initials?

8. Fry the jalebi for 2–3 minutes on each side until they're golden brown and crispy, then take them out of the oil using a slotted spoon. Allow the excess oil to drain off for 2–3 seconds, then add them straight into the warm sugar syrup. Make sure they soak up the syrup for 30 seconds to 1 minute.

9. Place the sugar-syrup-soaked jalebi onto a plate, ready to serve.

10. Fry the next batch of jalebi in the same way, and soak these in syrup too. (If you used a lemon wedge, you will see it become candied in the syrup . . . a bonus luscious treat!)

11. Enjoy while warm and crispy.

Now turn to page 68 or . . .
Catch up with the oldest, wisest grain (page 54)
to find out what's in store!

Gnocchi

Gnocchi are little potato-dough dumplings – often mistaken for pasta! Gnocchi are eaten everywhere, but were invented in the northern Italy, where it's colder and a better climate for growing potatoes rather than the traditional durum wheat for pasta. Although it's a very popular dish on menus, many people can't pronounce it. Try saying 'nyock-ee'. 'Gnocchi' is the plural, so if you only had one, it'd be a 'gnocco'.

Have a quick read of pages 19–21 before you try out this recipe.

4 servings (as a starter or accompaniment)
2 hours

560g floury potatoes
160g plain flour
¼ teaspoon salt, and a little more for boiling
Black pepper, to taste
Cold water, for boiling

1. Preheat the oven to 180°C (160°C fan).
2. Wash and dry the potatoes. Pierce a few holes in them using a fork or knife (to allow the steam to escape) and place them on a baking tray. Bake them in the oven for 40 minutes to 1 hour (turning them over halfway) until you can slide a fork into the skins and flesh easily. (You could bake the potatoes in the microwave on high for 7–8 minutes, turning them halfway. Remember to use a microwave-safe container.)
3. Leave the potatoes to cool enough so that you can peel them, then mash the potatoes in a bowl using a fork, masher or ricer. The potatoes must be mashed until very smooth.
4. Add the flour and salt and combine with the potatoes to create a soft dough using your hands. You can add the pepper here too, or sprinkle it on later after cooking. Don't overwork the dough by kneading it too much.
5. Split the dough into four and roll each one into thin, sausage-like shapes, about 25cm long and 2cm in diameter.
6. Cut the sausages into small 2cm portions – the gnocchi – and press and roll each gnocco down the back of a fork to make a little 'groovy' design.
7. Boil some water in a pan and add a little salt. Once the water has started to boil, add the gnocchi.
8. The gnocchi will sink to start with, but once they start to float, twirl them around in the water once or twice, then take them out using a slotted spoon, or drain using a colander. (See 'Steam' in the Glossary, page 75.)
9. Toss the cooked gnocchi into some sauce, or sprinkle with cheese and serve!

Now turn to page 68 or . . .
Pickle your best buds (page 58) and shout 'ahoj' to find out what's in store!

Potato Bread

Made using leftover potatoes, this flatbread or potato cake is often eaten for breakfast. As it's cut into quarters or 'farls', these can be known as potato farls, or as boxty (bacstaí in the Irish language), which probably relates to the Gaeilge words for baking or bakehouse. Potatoes (and potato bread!) are important to Ireland, and other countries, where the soil is good for growing starchy, nutritious, calorie-rich tubers.

Have a quick read of pages 19–21 before you try out this recipe.

8 farls

45 minutes

450g floury potatoes
Cold water, for boiling
110g self-raising flour, and a little extra for dusting
40g butter (or margarine), melted, and 15g for pan-frying
½ teaspoon salt
1 teaspoon black pepper (optional)
1–2 teaspoons chopped spring onions or herbs (optional)

1. Wash and peel the potatoes and add them to some cold water in a pan.
2. Bring to the boil, then reduce to a medium heat until you can slide a fork into the potato flesh easily. This takes about 20 minutes.
3. Take the potatoes out of the water using a slotted spoon and place them in a bowl to cool.
4. Mash the cooled potatoes using a fork or masher, then add the flour, melted butter and salt. Mix and knead this slightly to make a dough. Other ingredients you can mix in at this stage, if you wish, include black pepper, chopped spring onions or herbs.
5. Tip the dough out onto a floured surface and split it in half. Using a rolling pin, roll one half into a round pancake about 1cm thick and 15–16cm in diameter. Cut the round into 4 equal sections. Do the same with the other half of the dough.
6. Heat a large, non-stick frying pan over a medium heat and add a little butter to the pan.
7. Cook each quarter of the potato bread for 4–5 minutes on each side, making sure it's golden brown and cooked through. You might be able to fit 4 farls in the pan at the same time, so you can cook everything in 2 batches.
8. These taste great baked in the oven too: preheat the oven to 200°C (180°C fan) and cook for 15 minutes.

Now turn to page 68 or . . .
This friend will cry if we cry too (page 57), so find out what's in store!

33

Samosas

These triangular-shaped stuffed pastries originated in the Middle East – the name 'samosa' most probably came from the Persian name 'sanbosag', meaning 'pastry triangle'! Pretty much every culture has their very own version of a pastry filled with something delicious: pasties, empanadas, gyozas, kozhukattai, wontons . . . can you think of any others? This recipe is for baked Punjabi samosas, which can sit up on your plate, depending on your pastry folding skills!

Have a quick read of pages 19–21 before you try out this recipe.

16 samosas

1 hour 30 minutes

260g plain flour

¼ teaspoon salt

100g ghee, at room temperature

6–8 tablespoons (90–120ml) cold water

200–400g leftover curry (or try the bonus recipe, page 36)

Tip

Samosas are traditionally deep-fried until golden brown, so why not try that method sometime to compare results?

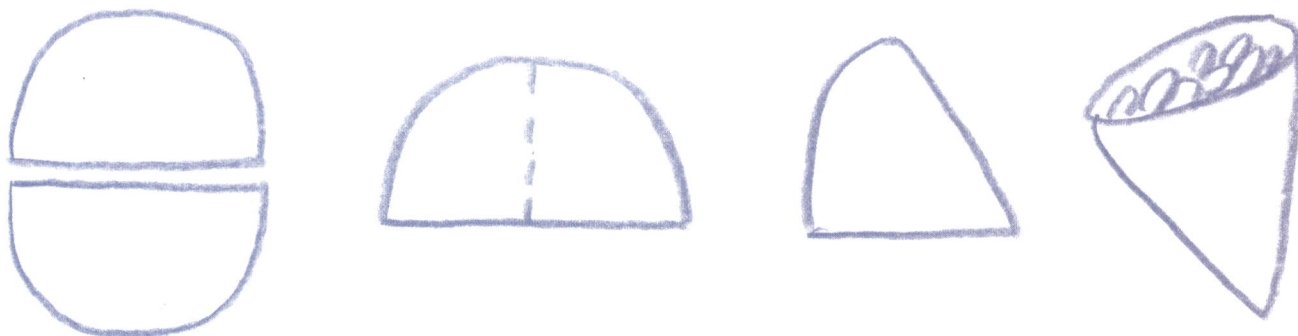

1. Put the flour and salt into a bowl and mix well.
2. Add 50g ghee into the flour and mix it in using your fingers so that the ghee isn't all in one place.
3. Add the water, a little at a time as you might not need it all. Mix with your hands until you have a firm pastry dough. Don't overwork or knead it too much.
4. Cover the dough with a clean tea towel and leave it to one side for 30–40 minutes.
5. Get your leftover curry ready – potato and pea curries go well in samosas – but you could use any fairly dry curry without too much sauce. Or try the bonus recipe (page 36). Alternatively, try grated cheese and chopped onions, or even a fruit filling!
6. Preheat the oven to 200°C (180°C fan). Line a baking tray.
7. Once the samosa dough is ready, split it into 8 equal balls, about 50g each. Leave the balls in the bowl, covered with the same tea towel as before.
8. Take a ball out and roll it into an oval shape on a smooth unfloured surface. It should be about 2mm thick and about 18 x 15cm.
9. Cut the oval in half widthways, so that you have 2 semi-circles.
10. Take one of the semi-circles and bring the two ends of the straight edge together, pinching and sticking them firmly together, so that you have a cone shape that you can hold gently in your hand like an ice cream cone. (You might need to moisten the pastry edges with a wet finger if it doesn't stick firmly together.)
11. Fill the cone with 2–3 teaspoons of the leftover curry, being careful not to add too much or too little. (You don't want them to burst during cooking, but they can't be all pastry with little going on inside either. It also depends on how thin you roll the pastry as to how much filling you can add.)
12. Bring the pastry cone edges together, overlapping them slightly, so that you form a triangle. Press the edges firmly to make sure no filling is peeking out. Do the same with the other semi-circle of dough. You now have 2 samosas.
13. Make the others in the same way and put them all on the baking tray.
14. Melt the rest of the ghee in the microwave (on high for 5–10 seconds) and brush over both sides of the samosas. Place into the preheated oven for 25–30 minutes, until golden brown. You may need to turn them over halfway through the cooking time.
15. Serve the samosas hot with a chutney or sauce of your choice!

Now turn to page 68 or . . .
There's someone who be-leafs in us (page 60),
so find out what's in store!

Samosa Curry

15 minutes

400g boiled, steamed or roasted potatoes
2 teaspoons vegetable or sunflower oil
½ teaspoon cumin seeds
½ teaspoon salt
100g cooked peas
½ teaspoon mustard seeds (optional)
¼ teaspoon turmeric powder (optional)

1. Cut the cooked potatoes into 1cm cubes. These could be leftover potatoes!
2. Heat the oil in a large, non-stick frying pan over a medium-high heat.
3. Once the oil is hot, add the cumin seeds and mustard seeds, if using. As these start to pop, add turmeric powder, if using, and salt.
4. Fry this for 30 seconds to 1 minute and add the potatoes and peas.
5. Mix well, heating through for 3–4 minutes, stirring gently, and leave to cool.

Tip

This is the perfect accompaniment for other recipes in this book, but if you want a more traditional Punjabi samosa filling, add kalonji (nigella) seeds, finely chopped ginger, green chillies, a sprinkling of aamchur (mango powder) or chaat masala, which adds a tangy flavour, or use lemon or lime juice instead.

Roti Canai

Pronounced 'cha-nigh', and also known as roti paratha, this flaky South Asian flatbread is a popular street food all over Malaysia, Singapore and Indonesia (and in Trinidad, known as 'Buss Up Shut'). Rotis can be eaten with fried eggs, curry gravy, dhal (lentil curry) or sugar. 'Roti' means 'bread' in Sanskrit (the ancient language of India), but there are different theories about the 'canai' part. It could refer to Chennai (Madras), channa (chickpea curry) or the Malay word meaning 'to roll thinly'.

Have a quick read of pages 19–21 before you try out this recipe.

8 rotis
1 hour, and 2 hours' resting time

420g plain flour, and a little extra for dusting
1 teaspoon salt
120ml ghee, melted, or vegetable oil
60ml condensed milk
240ml cold water

1. Sift the flour into a bowl, add the salt and sprinkle over 2 tablespoons (30ml) of ghee. Combine this gently with your fingers, rubbing the flour and ghee together.
2. Mix the condensed milk and water together in a measuring jug until they are completely combined.
3. Make a well in the centre of the flour mix, add the milk-water mixture and combine together to make a soft, sticky dough.
4. Add flour to your hands to stop the dough sticking, then knead the dough for 2–3 minutes in the bowl. Leave it in the bowl to rest, covered with a clean tea towel, for 40 minutes to an hour.
5. Split the dough into 8 balls, about 90g each, and leave them all in the bowl under the tea towel.
6. Take a ball and roll it out on a smooth surface, as thinly as possible, into a rectangle of about 30 x 20cm.
7. Brush some melted ghee on top of the very thin dough sheet and sprinkle some flour lightly on top.
8. Roll the sheet tightly, as if rolling a sheet of paper to make a solid tube.
9. Brush more ghee along the length of the roll, then coil it round, like a snail's shell.
10. Do the same with the other balls of dough, and place all the coils back in the bowl to rest for an hour.
11. After 1 hour, take each coil, one at a time, and press them out on a smooth surface to make round flatbreads (rotis), about 3–4mm thick and 16–18cm diameter. Brush both sides with a little ghee.
12. Heat a large, non-stick frying pan over a medium heat.
13. Place a roti on the pan and lightly fry each side for 2 minutes, until it puffs up slightly and has golden brown speckles all over.
14. Roti canai is very flaky, and this is achieved by transferring the cooked roti to a plate and squishing it! You may want to wrap the hot roti in a clean tea towel to protect your hands. Bring your hands together at either side of the hot roti, flat on the plate (be careful!) so that it squishes in between your hands, making it flaky.

Now turn to page 68 or . . .
Ask a lovely, happy rainbow (page 62)
to find out what's in store!

Crackers

These are thin pieces of crispy baked flatbread, perfect for topping with hummus, spreads and cheese. As crackers are dried and contain little water, mould can't grow on them, so they keep for a long time in an airtight container without spoiling. It's thought that crackers were invented thousands of years ago, when the Jewish people were escaping Egyptian slavery. With no time to wait for the bread to rise, the crispbreads, or matzoh, were completely flat when baked.

Have a quick read of pages 19–21 before you try out this recipe.

40 small crackers

40 minutes

100g plain flour, and a little extra for dusting

¼ teaspoon salt

25ml olive oil

50ml warm water

15g sesame seeds

1. Preheat the oven to 180°C (160°C fan). Line a large baking tray.
2. In a bowl, mix the flour and salt together, then mix in the olive oil with your fingers so that the oil isn't all in one place.
3. Add the water and mix well until you have a soft, sticky dough. Leave the dough in the bowl, covered with a clean tea towel, for 15 minutes.
4. Split the dough in half – it's easier to work with in two batches. Roll one piece of dough out on a floured surface until it's 2mm thick.
5. Sprinkle some sesame seeds on top and press these into the dough by rolling over the seeds and dough with the rolling pin.
6. Either cut the dough into small equal squares using a knife, or use a 4cm pastry cutter to make rounds; you can make other shapes, or even larger crackers, too.
7. Place all the shapes onto the baking tray and make holes in each cracker using a fork. This makes sure the crackers stay flat.
8. Use the other half of the dough to make more crackers, or store this in the fridge (for 1 week) or freezer (for up to 3 months) to use another time.
9. Bake the crackers in the oven for about 15 minutes, until they are lightly golden brown. Keep an eye on them so they don't brown too much.
10. Take the crackers out of the oven and leave them on the baking tray for 5 minutes, before placing them onto a wire rack to cool. Then enjoy!

Now turn to page 68 or . . .
Call upon the sweetest dust (page 53)
to find out what's in store!

Quesadillas

Quesadilla means 'little cheesy thing' in Spanish. Originating in Mexico, these are traditionally corn tortillas cooked on a comal (flat cast-iron griddle), sprinkled with grated cheese and folded in half, so the cheese melts and the tortilla becomes crispy. It's believed that in the sixteenth century, Spanish settlers in Mexico wanted to make turnovers and used tortillas instead of pastry.

Have a quick read of pages 19–21 before you try out this recipe.

12 tortillas
45 minutes

250g plain flour, and a little extra for dusting
2 tablespoons (30ml) olive or vegetable oil, and more for frying
½ teaspoon salt
150ml warm water
240g grated cheese (20g per tortilla), any cheese of your choice

1. Mix the flour, oil and salt in a bowl. Add the warm water and combine until you have a dough.
2. Knead the dough in the bowl or on a floured surface for 5–10 minutes, until you have a smooth ball of dough. Leave the dough to rest for 10–15 minutes in the bowl, covered with a clean tea towel.
3. Split the dough into 12 equal balls, about 35g each, dust them with flour and roll out into round tortillas about 2mm thick and 15–16cm in diameter.
4. Heat a large, non-stick frying pan over a medium-high heat until hot, and place a tortilla in the pan, dusting off any excess flour first. After 45 seconds to 1 minute, turn it over and cook the other side for another 45 seconds until it has golden brown spots all over. Take the tortilla out of the frying pan and wrap it in a clean tea towel to keep it warm.
5. Cook the other tortillas the same way, and add them to the tea towel, building up a pile of tortillas.
6. For the quesadillas, add a little oil to a clean frying pan over a medium-high heat, and add one tortilla.
7. Sprinkle grated cheese onto half of the tortilla, then fold the tortilla in half using a spatula or wooden spoon.
8. Press the tortilla down gently for 30 seconds to 1 minute, so the cheese melts (without oozing out) and the bottom of the quesadilla is crispy. Then turn it over and press down for another 30 seconds. Repeat with the remaining tortillas and cheese.
9. Cut the quesadillas into triangles, serve with guacamole, salsa and soured cream and enjoy!

Now turn to page 68 or . . .
A luscious herb (page 64) has a plan,
so find out what's in store!

Garlic Bread

Every culture has its own bread, as it's a good source of energy. Grain was first stone-ground to make flour, and mixed with water to form a flatbread like a chapatti or tortilla. It's thought that leavened (raised) bread was discovered accidentally, around 300 BC in Egypt, when yeast from the air fell on the dough. Garlic bread originated in Italy, where they rubbed olive oil and garlic on toasted bread. This basic bread dough recipe can be used to make buns, pizza bases, pides and so much more!

Have a quick read of pages 19–21 before you try out this recipe.

20 pieces
1 hour, and 2 hours' resting time

450g strong white bread or plain flour,
   and a little extra for dusting
2 teaspoons instant dried yeast
1 teaspoon salt
290ml warm water
4 tablespoons garlic butter (or 75g softened butter/
   margarine and 4 small cloves (10g) garlic, grated
   or finely chopped)
½ teaspoon chopped herbs, such as
   parsley or chives (optional)

1. Put the flour in a large bowl, then add the yeast to one side and the salt on the opposite side, so the yeast has chance to grow.
2. Make a well in the middle and add the warm water; the water shouldn't be too hot as this also stops the yeast working.
3. Bring the ingredients in the bowl together into a dough and start to knead it.
4. Transfer the dough to a lightly floured surface and knead for about 10 minutes until you have a smooth dough. Place it back in the bowl, covered with a clean tea towel, and leave it to double in size. This resting and rising time is known as 'proving' and should take about an hour.
5. If you don't already have garlic butter, in a small bowl mix the room temperature butter or margarine with the grated garlic. Other ingredients you can add at this stage include chopped herbs such as parsley or chives, if you'd like.
6. When the dough has doubled in size, knock or gently punch the dough.
7. Shape the dough into two 20cm long ovals and place on a floured baking tray, or place all the dough into a 900g/2lb (23 x 13 x 7cm) loaf tin. Cover with the tea towel and leave to prove again for 40 minutes.
8. Preheat the oven to 200°C (180°C fan), and when ready, place the dough into the oven. It should take 25–30 minutes for the bread to bake. You'll know it's ready when it's golden brown on top, and when you gently tap it you hear a hollow sound.
9. Carefully transfer the bread to a wire rack and leave to cool. (You could eat this bread as it is, or carry on and turn it into garlic bread!)
10. First, cut the bread into 2cm thick slices.
11. Lay the bread slices on a baking tray and spread them thinly with the garlic butter.
12. These garlic bread slices can be frozen like this to bake later, or can be baked straightaway in a preheated oven (180°C/160°C fan) for 8–10 minutes (or placed under a hot grill for 2–3 minutes), until the edges look crispy and golden brown.

Now turn to page 68 or . . .
Go for a spin with these greens (page 66)
to find out what's in store!

Steamed Buns

Originating in northern China, where it was easier to grow wheat than rice, steamed buns are famous for resembling soft little pillows. Traditionally, the buns, also known as mantou, bao, baozi or pau, can be filled with savoury (meat or vegetables) or sweet fillings (red bean paste or sweet custard).

There is a story about how these buns were invented. Chinese Chancellor Zhuge Liang, responsible for planning military operations, had to lead his army across a river, but was told of a legend. To get across safely, he needed to sacrifice the heads of 50 of his soldiers to the river gods. Zhuge wasn't prepared to lose any men, so they filled 50 balls of dough with meat and threw them into the river as 'human heads'. The plan worked and the army crossed the river safely.

Have a quick read of pages 19–21 before you try out this recipe.

4 large or 8 small buns
1 hour, and 2 hours' resting time

2 teaspoons instant dried yeast
165ml warm water
220g strong white bread or plain flour
2 tablespoons powdered milk
1 teaspoon salt
4–8 chocolate pieces (optional,
    for sweet buns)
4 tablespoons stir-fried
    vegetables (optional,
    for savoury buns)

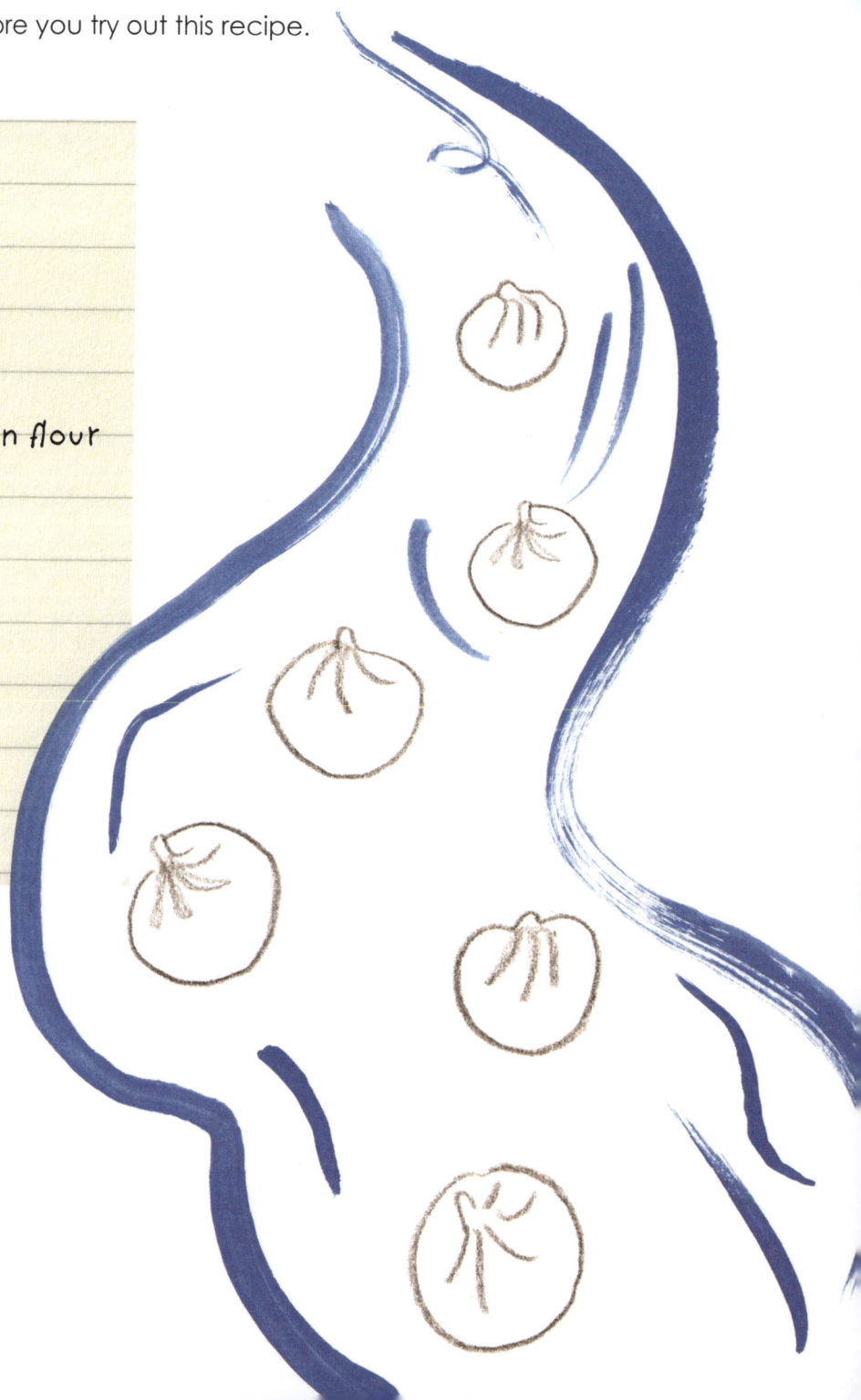

1. In a bowl, mix the yeast with 2–3 tablespoons of the warm water and a tablespoon of flour to form a paste. Leave this to one side for 15–20 minutes.
2. Add the rest of the warm water, flour, powdered milk and salt, and mix well to make a dough.
3. Knead the dough in the bowl or on a work surface for about 10 minutes until the dough is soft and elastic.
4. Return the dough to the bowl, cover with a clean tea towel, and leave to one side for about 1 hour until the dough has doubled in size.
5. Once the dough has doubled in size, knock or gently punch the dough, then bring it together into a ball and split it into 4 large (about 100g each) or 8 small (about 50g each) balls.
6. When unfilled, these buns are called mantou. At this stage you could flatten each ball and add a stuffing of your choice, such as chocolate or stir-fried vegetables, then roll them back into balls ready for steaming. They are now known as bao!
7. Place each ball onto a square of greaseproof paper (about 10 x 10cm) and leave them to rise under a large container or bowl for 40–50 minutes until they have doubled in size.
8. Get a steamer ready, or use a large pan or wok with some water in it and a wire rack on top and bring the water to a boil. Make sure the water doesn't boil over the rack as you'll end up with soggy buns. (You'll have to cover the buns when steaming, so you'll need a lid that covers the pan and the buns without squishing the buns.)
9. Once the water has started to boil, turn the heat down to a simmer and gently place 2–3 buns with their papers into the steamer or onto the wire rack, with 3–4cm of space in between each bun as they will expand.
10. The buns should take 6–8 minutes to steam. When the tops have a soft, sticky skin, they're ready. Transfer them gently to a serving dish, then steam the next batch of buns in the same way. Plain buns without stuffing can be served cut in half and filled with anything of your choice. These are now known as gua bao.

Now turn to page 68 or . . .
Pick this pal from a palm (page 52) to find out what's in store!

Stollen

You chose Marzipan, who can help make Stollen. Marzipan is a soft, sweet paste made from ground almonds. Leonardo da Vinci once made marzipan sculptures, but wasn't too amused that the courtiers in Milan gobbled them all up so quickly!

Stollen is a 'cake-bread', as the dough contains yeast, but is rich with sugar and fruits like a cake, and often contains marzipan and candied citrus fruit peel. Every Christmas in Dresden, Germany, there is a Stollenfest, where the famous Dresdner Christstollen is paraded through the city in a ceremonial carriage.

This recipe is for stollen bites, using the scone recipe (page 22), so there's no need for proving!

Have a quick read of pages 19–21 before you try out this recipe.

14–16 stollen bites

45 minutes

350g self-raising flour, and a little extra for dusting

85g caster sugar

85g cold margarine (or butter)

75g raisins

175ml milk

110g marzipan (see bonus recipe, page 45)

1 teaspoon mixed spice (optional)

Icing sugar (optional)

1. Preheat the oven to 220°C (190°C fan).
2. Make the stollen dough in the same way as the scones (page 22). As there's no need to brush these with milk, use all of the milk in the dough. You could also add mixed spice to make it taste more Christmassy, if you'd like!
3. Bring the dough together on a floured board or surface and split it in half. Flatten or roll each dough portion into squares about 1cm thick and 15 x 15cm.
4. Roll the marzipan into 2 logs (it's easier to roll on a surface dusted with icing sugar), about 15cm in length and 2cm in diameter, and place each log at one end of each dough square.
5. Roll the dough around the marzipan so that the marzipan is covered. Cut each stollen log into 7–8 bite-sized pieces, each about 2cm wide.
6. Place the pieces onto a lined baking tray, equally spaced, and bake for 12–15 minutes, until golden brown.
7. Dust them with icing sugar to make them look snowy, if you'd like.

make your own
marzipan

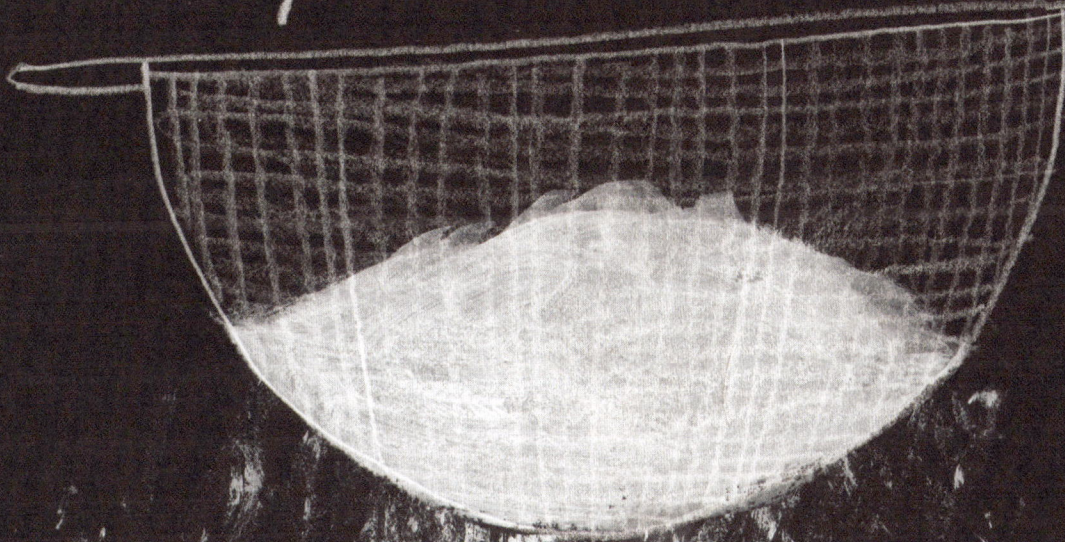

10–15 minutes

30g icing sugar
80g ground almonds
2 teaspoons water
½ teaspoon almond
essence

1. Sift the icing sugar into a bowl, add the ground almonds and mix well.
2. Add the water and almond essence, and use your hands to bring everything together into a dough. This can be rolled into logs, wrapped in greaseproof paper and kept in the fridge for up to 1 week until you're ready to use.

Now turn to page 68.

Chocolate Cheesecake

You chose Silken Tofu, who can help you make a Chocolate Cheesecake. Often cheesecakes are made with a soft cheese, but how about trying something a little different? Tofu is soya bean curd made from soya milk. Silken tofu is a popular breakfast dish in Japan and is so soft and creamy, unlike regular tofu. Cheesecakes might feel like a modern American dessert, but they date back to Ancient Greece, where they were made of cheese, wheat flour and honey!

Have a quick read of pages 19–21 before you try out this recipe.

10 servings
40 minutes, and overnight
   setting time

5 chocolate chip cookies,
   about 170g (page 23)
25g margarine (or butter)
2 x 300g packs of silken tofu
300g chocolate chips or pieces

For the base (optional)
40g margarine (or butter)
40g caster sugar
2 teaspoons (10ml) milk
60g self-raising flour
1 teaspoon cocoa powder, sifted

Tip

Dark chocolate helps the silken tofu set because it contains more cocoa butter, which is solid at room temperature, with little or none of the dairy fat of milk chocolate, which is softer at room temperature. Using pure dark chocolate can taste bitter, as there's little sugar or dairy, so you'll need a chocolate that sets well *and* tastes good!

1. Crumble the prepared cookies into a bowl with your fingers, or crush them gently with a rolling pin, so they look like breadcrumbs.
2. Melt the margarine in a pan over a low heat and stir in the cookie crumbs.
3. Press the mixture into the base of a lined 20cm diameter cake tin and keep it in the fridge to cool. Continue from Step 9.

To make the base (optional)

4. If you haven't any leftover cookies, preheat the oven to 200°C (180°C fan).
5. Cream the margarine and sugar in a bowl, using a fork, as before (page 23).
6. Add the milk, then the flour, and mix well until you have a cookie dough. If you'd like a crunchier base to your cheesecake, leave out the milk. And to make the cheesecake double-chocolatey, add the cocoa powder.
7. Press the mixture into the base of a lined 20cm diameter cake tin. It may look like a thin layer, but it will rise.
8. Bake this cheesecake base for 15–20 minutes, until golden brown. Leave to cool.

To make the cheesecake

9. Drain the water from the silken tofu, add the tofu to a blender, and blend until it is creamy. (If you don't have a blender or liquidiser, mash batches of the tofu really well with a fork or a hand whisk, to make it as soft, creamy and smooth as possible.) Leave this to one side.
10. Add some water to a pan and find a bowl that sits on top of the pan, making sure the bottom of the bowl doesn't touch the water.
11. Add the chocolate chips to the bowl and leave the bowl to one side.
12. Heat the pan of water over a medium heat until the water is about to boil. Reduce the heat, put the bowl of chocolate chips over the hot water in the pan, and stir until all the chocolate has melted. Make sure the chocolate doesn't overheat and become lumpy and grainy. (If easier, microwave the chocolate in the bowl on a low or defrost setting in 10–20-second bursts, giving it a good stir in between until all the chocolate has melted.)
13. Now, before the chocolate can cool down, add the blended tofu, a little at a time, stirring quickly to combine it all together over the heat.
14. Pour the chocolate-tofu mixture over the base in the cake tin and spread it evenly.
15. Keep it in the fridge for a minimum of 5 hours (overnight is best), cut into slices and enjoy!

Now turn to page 68.

Appelbeignets

You chose Sparkling Water, who can help you make Appelbeignets. The carbon dioxide gas bubbles that make the water fizzy and sparkly help create light, crispy batters. Lemonade works too.

Appelbeignets are enjoyed during New Year's Eve celebrations. The Dutch also have a puff-pastry treat called Appelflappen, and often the two names are mixed up! Whatever the name, these are apple-solutely scrummy.

Have a quick read of pages 19–21 before you try out this recipe.

16–18 appelbeignets

30 minutes

200g apples
100g self-raising flour
20g caster sugar
1 teaspoon powdered ginger
140ml sparkling water
2 tablespoons margarine (or butter), or 450ml oil for frying
Icing sugar (optional)

Tip

Appelbeignets are fluffier and crispier when deep-fried in oil, so why not try that sometime to compare results?

1. Peel and core the apples, then slice them into ½cm thick slices. Dry them using a piece of kitchen roll, as this will help the batter stick to the apples.
2. In a bowl, whisk together the flour, sugar, ginger and sparkling water until you have a smooth batter, not too runny and not too thick, with no lumps.
3. Place a large, non-stick frying pan over a medium heat.
4. Add a little margarine and swirl the pan so the base is coated. Pan-frying in margarine or butter adds flavour, but at high temperatures these can burn, so keep an eye on the heat. Another option is to shallow-fry in 1cm depth of oil.
5. Dip each slice of apple into the batter and place into the frying pan. You should be able to fit 4 coated apple slices in the pan at a time.
6. After 2–3 minutes, the batter should start to expand slightly, crisp and turn golden brown. Turn the slices over and cook for another 2–3 minutes.
7. Transfer the slices to a plate lined with kitchen roll.
8. Shallow-fry the rest of the apple slices in the same way, dust them with icing sugar, if using, and enjoy while warm.

Now turn to page 68.

Anzac Biscuits

You chose Rolled Oats, who can help you make Anzac Biscuits. They're called 'rolled oats' because they've been steamed and flattened under high-pressure rollers. It is believed that these sweet Anzac biscuits were sent to Australian and New Zealand Army Corps (ANZAC) soldiers during World War One as a reminder of how much those at home loved and missed them. But most Anzac biscuits were actually sold at fundraising events to raise money to help win the war.

Have a quick read of pages 19–21 before you try out this recipe.

12 biscuits
30–40 minutes

150g margarine (or butter)
80g golden syrup
150g self-raising flour
150g caster or Demerara sugar
1 teaspoon powdered ginger
   (for a punchy flavour) or
3 tablespoons (15g) of
   desiccated coconut (optional)
110g rolled oats

1. Preheat the oven to 180°C (160°C fan). Line two baking trays.
2. Add the margarine and golden syrup to a small pan over a medium heat. Stir until everything melts into a gorgeous golden liquid, then take the pan off the heat and leave it to one side.
3. In a bowl, mix the flour, sugar, ginger or desiccated coconut, if using, and oats together.
4. Pour the melted mixture into the bowl with the dry ingredients and mix everything together well.
5. Take 2 heaped teaspoons of the mixture (about 50g) and roll it between your palms into a ball. Put this ball onto a lined baking tray.
6. Repeat with the rest of the mixture and place all the balls onto the baking trays.
7. Flatten each ball with the back of a teaspoon into a round biscuit about 1cm thick and 7cm in diameter. Leave some space between the biscuits as they will spread during baking. (Freezing the biscuits before baking makes them spread less, as the fat becomes solid in the freezer, so doesn't melt and spread as quickly when baked.)
8. Bake for 12–15 minutes, until golden brown, then leave to cool on a wire rack.
9. Your crunchy yet chewy Anzac biscuits are ready to enjoy!

miss
you

Now turn to page 68.

Maamoul

You chose Dates, who can help you make maamoul. The name 'date' is from the Greek word 'daktulous' (δάκτυλος) meaning 'finger', as they're long fruits. Maamoul or ma'amoul are cookies from the Levant area in the Middle East made with flour or semolina and filled with either dates, walnuts or pistachios. They're moulded with wooden moulds, or tabbeh. So it isn't a surprise that maamoul have different shapes depending on what's inside: date maamoul are usually disc-shaped.

Maamoul are eaten at Eid or Easter to celebrate the end of fasting during Ramadan or Lent, as well as during Purim and Rosh Hashanah.

Have a quick read of pages 19–21 before you try out this recipe.

8 maamoul
1 hour

3 tablespoons (45ml)
  vegetable oil
3 teaspoons caster sugar
½ teaspoon cinnamon
140g self-raising flour
4 tablespoons (60ml) water
130g dates, pitted
Icing sugar (optional)

1. Whisk 40ml of oil, the sugar and the cinnamon together in a bowl.
2. Add the flour and rub together with your fingers until it's a bit like wet sand.
3. Add the water and bring everything together into a mouldable, soft dough. Leave the dough in the fridge to rest for 15–20 minutes.
4. Chop the dates into small pieces (they'll be very sticky!).
5. Try moulding the chopped dates into 8 small balls using your hands. Each ball should be about 15g. If they're too sticky, rub a little of the leftover oil on your hands. If the dates aren't sticky enough, microwave them for 15–20 seconds on high.
6. Preheat the oven to 200°C (180°C fan).
7. Take the maamoul dough out of the fridge and make 8 balls out of this, too. Each ball should weigh about 30g.
8. Take a ball of maamoul dough and flatten it in the palm of one hand. Cup your hand so that you turn the dough into a small bowl shape. Pop one of the date balls inside and close up the dough around it. Make sure none of the date mixture is peeping out.
9. You now have a ball of dough with dates inside. Flatten each ball slightly to make them disc-shaped and place each disc equally spaced (1–2cm apart) on a lined baking tray. Why not use a fork to make pretty designs on the top, too?
10. Bake them for 14–15 minutes, until lightly browned.
11. Transfer them carefully to a wire rack to cool, dust with icing sugar while still a little warm, if you'd like, and enjoy!

Now turn to page 68.

Heuningkoek

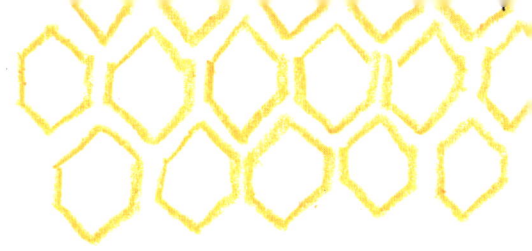

You chose Honey, who can help you make Heuningkoek (pronounced 'heur-ning-cook'). Bees pollinate plants while collecting nectar. By drinking the nectar, digesting it and taking it back to the hive where they pass it mouth-to-mouth to other bees, the runny nectar turns into thick honey.

In Afrikaans, Heuningkoek means both 'honeycomb' and 'honey cake' as the poked holes make this South African treat look like honeycomb! It's thought the Ancient Greeks invented this as a sweet offering to the gods, and today in Greece there are many similar honey-drizzled cakes. In the seventeenth century, the Dutch honingkoek (or ontbijtkoek), which is actually baked with honey, was sold in bakeries during Sinterklaas celebrations.

Have a quick read of pages 19–21 before you try out this recipe.

8–10 servings
1 hour

225g caster sugar
4 tablespoons (60ml)
   vegetable oil, and a little
   extra for greasing
340ml water
1 teaspoon vanilla extract
340g self-raising flour
6 tablespoons (90ml) honey
   (or 4 tablespoons (60ml)
   honey and 60g butter or
   margarine)

1. Preheat the oven to 200°C (180°C fan). Grease and line a 20cm cake tin.
2. Make the vanilla cupcake mixture as before (page 27), but this time pour the batter into the cake tin. Bake for 40–45 minutes, or until a dinner knife or toothpick comes out clean and dry when pushed into the middle of the cake.
3. Just before the cake comes out of the oven, melt the honey in the microwave on high in 10-second bursts until it's a runny liquid. For a richer honey sauce, melt and stir the honey and butter for 3–4 minutes in a pan over a medium heat until nicely combined.
4. Take the cake out of the oven and, while it's still in the tin, make lots of holes in the top of the cake using a fork. Pour or spoon the melted honey (or honey sauce) over the cake. Serve while warm.

Tip

If you have spare vanilla cupcakes, why not turn them into heuningkoek cupcakes by making holes in the tops and pouring on some honey sauce?

Now turn to page 68.

Lolo Buns

You chose Coconut Milk, who can help you make Lolo Buns. In Fiji, coconut milk is called 'lolo'.

Coconuts are fruits not nuts, and we get coconut milk by scraping the flesh from inside the mature coconut and squeezing it in water. Many cultures enjoy various forms of 'milky bun', such as shokupan in Japan. But when there are coconuts, why not make coconut milk buns? In Samoa and Hawaii, these buns sit in a sweet coconut sauce and are called panipopo ('pani' for 'bread' and 'popo' for 'coconut').

Have a quick read of pages 19–21 before you try out this recipe.

6 buns
30 minutes, and 2 hours' resting time

1 teaspoon instant dried yeast
220g strong white bread or plain
   flour, and a little extra for dusting
1 tablespoon powdered milk
1 teaspoon salt
165ml warm water
130ml coconut milk
Sugar, to taste (optional)

1. In a bowl, add the yeast, flour, powdered milk and salt.
2. Add the warm water and bring it all together, kneading the dough in the bowl or on a floured surface for 5–6 minutes until it's smooth and stretchy.
3. Place the dough back into the bowl, covered with a plate or clean tea towel, and leave it somewhere warm to prove for an hour.
4. After 1 hour, the dough should have doubled in size. Knock or gently punch the dough, then split it into 6 equal balls (about 65g each).
5. Place the balls in a flower shape (5 petals with a centre) in a deep 20cm-diameter cake tin (make sure it isn't a loose-bottomed tin!) and leave to rise for 40 minutes.
6. Preheat the oven to 200°C (180°C fan).
7. Pour the coconut milk over the top of the proved dough balls and put them in the oven. For a sweeter flavour, add 1–2 teaspoons of sugar to the coconut milk.
8. Bake for 20–25 minutes, until golden brown. You'll see that most of the coconut milk has been absorbed into the buns, leaving a little 'coconut sauce' at the bottom of the tin.
9. Leave to cool for 5–10 minutes and serve warm!

Now turn to page 68.

Linga Cookies

You chose Icing Sugar, who can help you make Linga Cookies. Icing sugar is also known as powdered sugar, as it is ground up to a fine powder. It's used to make icing for cakes and biscuits, and to lightly dust treats so they look snowy. 'Linga' or 'longa', depending on the region in the Philippines, is the word for 'sesame seeds'. These cookies are circular or oval and often dipped in hot drinks such as tsokolate, a Filipino hot chocolate drink, famous at breakfast, meryenda (afternoon snacks) and at Pasko (Christmas time).

Have a quick read of pages 19–21 before you try out this recipe.

12 cookies
30 minutes

50g icing sugar
A pinch of salt
3 tablespoons (45ml) light olive oil
3 tablespoons (45ml) warm water
130g self-raising flour
25g sesame seeds

1. Preheat the oven to 200°C (180°C fan). Line a baking tray.
2. Sift the icing sugar into a bowl. Add the salt, oil and water and whisk together.
3. Add the flour and fold in until you have a soft, mouldable dough.
4. Split the dough into 12 equal balls, about 20–25g each.
5. Sprinkle the sesame seeds onto a plate and coat the dough balls in the seeds.
6. On the plate, flatten each ball using the palm of your hand or the back of a tablespoon to turn them into disc shapes. You'll automatically press the sesame seeds firmly into the dough. Alternatively, to make oval cookies, you can roll the balls into sausage shapes, then flatten each one. Place the cookies onto the baking tray.
7. Bake for 15 minutes, until they're golden brown. Leave to cool on a wire rack and then enjoy!

Tip

As the climate is humid in the Philippines, olive trees from which to harvest olive oil can't be grown. Usually, a shortening, or a solid fat made from liquid vegetable oil, is used. So why not try using butter, margarine or even melted coconut oil in this recipe instead?

Now turn to page 68.

Injera

You chose Teff Flour, who can help you make Injera. Teff is an ancient grain from Ethiopia, which means it hasn't changed much over the years. It is the smallest grain in the world: one wheat seed is the same size as 100 teff seeds!

A popular soft, thin pancake called injera is made in Ethiopia and Eritrea. It is usually eaten with spicy lentils and other delicious accompaniments on top, and everyone sits around it to share from the same plate. True injera batter is fermented for 3–4 days. The recipe here is quicker, and because injera is a vegan dish we're speeding up the fermentation with soya yoghurt, but you can use dairy yoghurt too!

Have a quick read of pages 19–21 before you try out this recipe.

8–10 small injera
45 minutes

45g plain flour
90g teff flour
A pinch of sugar
½ teaspoon baking powder
70g soya (or dairy) yoghurt
145ml water (to make sure the batter is runny enough)
1 tablespoon vegetable or sunflower oil
A pinch of salt (optional)

1. Put the plain flour, teff flour, sugar and baking powder into a bowl and mix well. (You could also add a pinch of salt to balance the sweetness, if you'd like.)
2. In another bowl or measuring jug, whisk up the yoghurt and water.
3. Make a well in the dry ingredients and pour the runny yoghurt mixture into this. Whisk until you have a batter with no lumps, then leave this to one side for 10 minutes. (For a more flavoursome injera, leave the batter overnight in a warm place, and when you're ready to use it, whisk it up again, mixing in any liquid that has formed on the top. Add the salt after fermenting, to give the natural yeast a chance to work.)
4. Place a large, non-stick frying pan over a medium-high heat and add a teaspoon of oil. Swirl the pan around gently so that the base is coated in oil, and heat until the oil is hot.
5. Using a ladle or a measuring jug, pour 2–3 tablespoons of the injera batter into the centre of the frying pan. Swirl the pan gently or use the back of the ladle to spread the batter in circular movements to make a thin pancake about 15cm in diameter.
6. Cook the injera for 2–3 minutes, or until the top doesn't look raw or runny anymore and you see bubbles appear and pop. The edges will look deep golden brown and crispy. And just like the dosas of southern India, injera aren't flipped.
7. Serve the first injera and continue to make the rest in the same way, adding a little oil whenever needed to make sure they don't stick.
8. Injera are best eaten as soon as they're made.

Tip

Injera taste neither sweet nor sour, so leaving the batter overnight helps to develop the flavour. Using only teff flour gives the injera a deep brown colour and richer flavour, and means they're gluten-free, too. If teff's tough to find, why not try another flour? While it won't be quite the same, you can still practise your injera-making skills!

Now turn to page 68.

Socca

You chose Chickpea Flour, who can help you make Socca. Also known as Bengal gram or *Cicer arietinum*, the humble chickpea is eaten all over the world in falafels, channa masala and hummus. Dishes known as socca, cade or panisse in the south of France are pancake-like flatbreads traditionally made with chickpea flour (ground-up dried chickpeas), water and oil and baked in a very hot oven. Dried chickpeas can be planted just like beans, but chickpea plant leaves and flowers are cuter! Why not give it a go?

Have a quick read of pages 19–21 before you try out this recipe.

2 socca

40 minutes

80g chickpea flour

165ml water

1 tablespoon plain flour

A pinch of sugar (optional for sweet-ness, if you're not using carrots)

½ teaspoon baking powder

2 tablespoons (30ml) oil, and

   2 teaspoons (10ml) oil for frying

30g grated carrots, or any other vegetable of your choice

Salt and pepper, to taste (optional)

1. In a large mixing bowl, make the chickpea batter by whisking up the chickpea flour and water. Sprinkle in the plain flour, sugar (if using) and baking powder, and whisk it well, making sure there are no lumps. The baking powder and flour help create a fluffier, bread-like socca.
2. Add 2 tablespoons of oil and whisk again. Leave the batter to one side for 20 minutes.
3. Place a large, non-stick frying pan over a medium-high heat. Add 1 teaspoon of oil and swirl the pan so the base is coated in oil.
4. Take the bowl of chickpea batter and add the grated carrot (or other vegetable). Mix well.
5. Using a measuring jug to help, pour half of this mixture into the frying pan. Swirl the pan to help the mixture spread out into a thin layer, and cook it for 1–2 minutes until the top looks less runny and the bottom looks crispy.
6. Flip the socca and cook on the other side for another 1–2 minutes until that side is crispy and golden too.
7. Use the rest of the batter to make another socca in the same way.
8. Sprinkle salt and pepper over the top, if you'd like, and serve!

Now turn to page 68.

Röstis and Latkes

You chose Onions, who can help you make Röstis and Latkes. Onions release a chemical when cut that irritates the tear glands in our eyes, making us cry.

Röstis and latkes are crispy potato fritters. In Switzerland, röstis are often fried in butter and eaten for breakfast. Many celebrations around the world involve feasting, including the eight-day celebration of Hanukkah. Oil-based foods, such as latkes, help remember the Temple's menorah, which was alight for eight days and nights when there was only enough oil to burn for one day.

Have a quick read of pages 19–21 before you try out this recipe.

8–10 röstis or latkes

40 minutes

200g potatoes
50g onion, finely chopped
   or grated
2–3 teaspoons plain flour
1 teaspoon salt
A sprinkling of cold water
30g butter, or
   30ml vegetable or
sunflower oil

1. There's no need to peel the potatoes, just wash them well, then grate them.
2. Put the grated potatoes and onion into a clean tea towel or cheesecloth, bundle the ends together and squeeze out all the water from the vegetables over a bowl.
3. If you have enough liquid, leave it in the bowl and you may see the potato starch settle at the bottom (it'll be a milkier liquid than what's on top). Using a little of this potato starch in the next step can help bind the potatoes and onions together, and it's always nice to use things that might otherwise have been thrown away.
4. Put the potatoes and onions in a bowl and mix in 2 teaspoons of flour and the salt. Use a teaspoon to add a sprinkling of water and a little of the potato starch too. The potatoes and onions should stick together thanks to the flour and water, but you might need to add a little more of each if they don't. The less water, the crispier the potatoes!
5. For latkes, sometimes crushed matzoh (flatbreads traditionally eaten during Passover) are used instead of flour.
6. Place a large, non-stick frying pan over a medium heat.
7. Add the butter or oil to the pan and swirl the pan so that it coats the base. Remember, oil is important during Hanukkah if you're making latkes! (If using butter, keep an eye on the heat, as the milk in butter can start to burn.)
8. Take 1–2 tablespoons of the potato mixture and place it carefully into the pan. Flatten it down with the back of the spoon. You should be able to fit 4–5 in the pan at the same time without overcrowding them, as you'll need space to turn them over.
9. Lightly fry them for 1–2 minutes on each side until crispy and golden brown. Transfer each one to a plate lined with a piece of kitchen roll.
10. Finish making the rest, and serve while warm and crispy!

Now turn to page 68.

Lokše

You chose Sauerkraut, who can help you make Lokše (pronounced 'lok-shey'; singular is lokša, 'lok-sha'), which are potato flatbreads from Slovakia. They're eaten as a light snack or accompaniment, and popular during harvest time and at Christmas markets. Lokše are filled with anything sweet or savoury, but traditionally with sauerkraut, or fermented cabbage. Fermentation makes the cabbage tangy and sour so Slovaks call it 'kyslá kapusta' (sour cabbage). Norway's lefse is a similar flatbread, served with butter and sprinkles of sugar and cinnamon.

Have a quick read of pages 19–21 before you try out this recipe.

15 lokše

1 hour 30 minutes

2 teaspoons salt
Cold water, for boiling
450g waxy potatoes
150g plain flour, and a little
   extra for dusting
Black pepper, to taste
2 tablespoons (30ml) melted
   butter or oil (optional)
Sauerkraut (see bonus recipe,
   page 59)

1. Add 1 teaspoon of salt to a pan of cold water.
2. Wash the potatoes and add them to the pan. Using waxy potatoes makes them easier to grate later.
3. Boil the potatoes for 15–20 minutes, until you can just push a fork into them, but they don't need to be so soft that you can mash them.
4. Drain the potatoes and leave them to cool enough so that you can peel them. Then, using a grater, grate the potatoes into a bowl.
5. Add the flour and the rest of the salt to the grated potatoes and knead this in the bowl for 3–4 minutes to form a dough. It should all come together, but if it's too dry and crumbly, add a sprinkling of water, and if too wet add more flour.
6. Split the dough into 15 balls, about 35–40g each, and leave them in the bowl to rest for 10 minutes.
7. Roll each ball out on a well-floured surface into a round flatbread about 3–4mm thick and 12–13cm in diameter.
8. Place a large, non-stick frying pan over a medium heat.
9. Cook each lokša in a dry pan for 2–3 minutes on each side. You'll see golden brown spots underneath when you peek, which means that side is cooked and it's ready to flip over. Each lokša will puff up slightly, and as it fills with hot air you'll know the inside is perfectly cooked.
10. Place them on a plate, and brush each one with some melted butter or oil, if you'd like.
11. Fill them with sauerkraut, sprinkle with some pepper, then roll them up like a pancake and enjoy!

Sauerkraut

While Slovaks once made huge amounts of sauerkraut in giant wooden barrels to last the winter, squishing the cabbage with their feet, we'll stick to a smaller amount in this recipe, which you can squeeze with your hands!

1. Place the cabbage into a bowl and sprinkle the salt on top.
2. Using your hands, squeeze the cabbage and salt together for a minute or two. Stop for 2–3 minutes then repeat the squeezing. The salt pulls out all the water from the cabbage as the cells break down, releasing sugars that the good bacteria will feed on. The bacteria, which live naturally on many vegetables, including cabbages, release natural acids which give the tangy taste and preserve the cabbage. This leaking cabbage water is the salty brine that the cabbage will ferment in.
3. Make sure the cabbage is completely covered by the brine by pushing it down into the bowl with a spoon. Or place a saucer with a weight (such as a full jam jar) on top to keep the cabbage pressed down. It will take 3–4 hours for the cabbage to be fully covered, so keep checking. Cover the whole thing loosely with a clean tea towel, so that air can flow in and out.
4. Check the cabbage every day, making sure it's still covered by the brine. You can stir it from time to time, and even taste it. At warmer temperatures fermentation is faster, so your sauerkraut might be ready before you know it.
5. After 3 days at room temperature, you'll have sauerkraut! You could leave it for longer (up to 10 days) for a really sour sauerkraut.
6. Transfer the sauerkraut to a clean jar and store it in the fridge. Traditional Korean kimchi is made in a similar way.

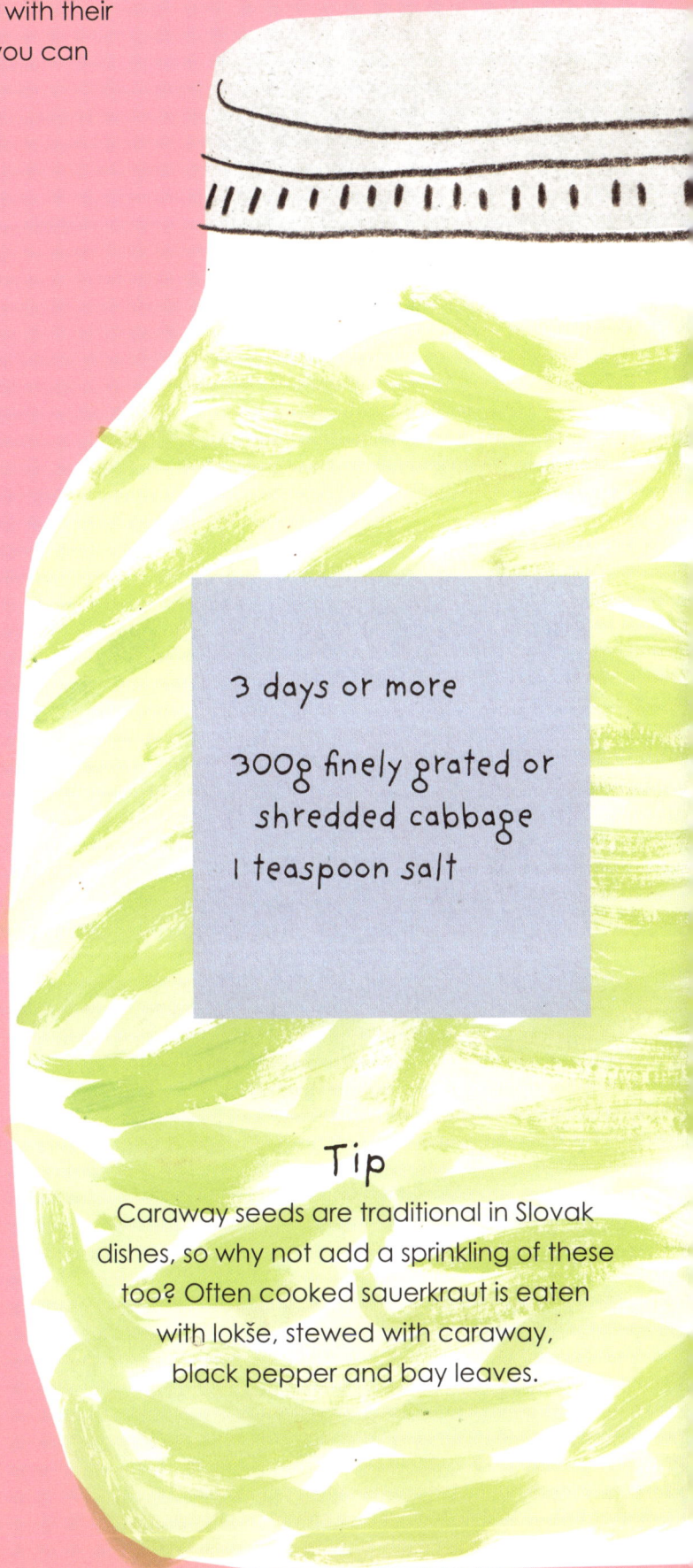

3 days or more

300g finely grated or shredded cabbage
1 teaspoon salt

Tip

Caraway seeds are traditional in Slovak dishes, so why not add a sprinkling of these too? Often cooked sauerkraut is eaten with lokše, stewed with caraway, black pepper and bay leaves.

Now turn to page 68.

Stuffed Paratha

You chose Fenugreek Leaves, who can help you make Stuffed Parathas. In Punjabi, potato is 'aloo', fenugreek is 'methi', layers is 'parat' and flour is 'atta'. Aloo methi paratha is a popular northern Indian breakfast flatbread stuffed with potato and fenugreek leaves. But you can use anything to make a stuffed paratha, including fresh coriander leaves and leftover curry (see bonus recipe on page 61).

Have a quick read of pages 19–21 before you try out this recipe.

4 stuffed parathas
1 hour

250g plain, wholemeal or chapatti flour, and a little extra for dusting
175ml water, at room temperature
Salt, to taste
1 teaspoon dried fenugreek leaves
200g leftover curry (or see bonus recipe, page 61)
25g ghee

1. Mix the flour, water and salt together in a bowl until you have a sticky dough. You can sprinkle in the dried fenugreek leaves here and mix well, or add them into the leftover curry filling later. If you want to use fresh leaves, see the bonus recipe on page 61.
2. Cover the dough and leave it to rest for 15 minutes.
3. Knead the dough in the bowl for 2–3 minutes, adding a little extra flour if it's still sticky, until it becomes smooth. Cover the bowl again and put it into the fridge for 30 minutes.
4. Split the dough into 4 equal balls, about 100g each.
5. If not added earlier, add the fenugreek leaves to the dry leftover curry. Mash it all together with a fork. Divide the mashed curry into 4 equal parts, about 50g each, and roll these into balls.
6. Flatten one ball of dough in the palm of one hand. Cup your hand so that you turn the dough into a small bowl shape. The dough bowl should have a thicker bottom than the sides. Pop a ball of curry inside and close up the dough around it. Make sure none of the curry is peeping out.
7. Do the same with the rest of the dough balls.
8. Roll each stuffed dough ball on a floured surface into round flatbreads about 5mm thick and 16–17cm in diameter. Roll them very gently so that the stuffing doesn't pop out.
9. Place a large, non-stick frying pan over a medium heat.
10. Cook the first paratha in a dry pan for 2–3 minutes. Then turn it over and use the back of a teaspoon to spread a sprinkling of ghee over the top and cook for another 2 minutes. Flip it over again for another 2 minutes, adding another sprinkling of ghee.
11. As the paratha cooks you will see little golden brown spots. The paratha will puff up slightly, and as it fills with hot air, you'll know the dough is fully cooked.
12. Transfer it to a plate and cook the other parathas in the same way. Enjoy with butter, raita (yoghurt mixed with shredded vegetables such as cucumber), yoghurt with a sprinkling of toasted, ground cumin seeds, or a chutney or pickle of your choice!

Tip

If you haven't enough leftover curry or it's not dry enough, add a small boiled potato or two and mash it all together.

Stuffed Paratha Curry

15 minutes

200g boiled or steamed potatoes
2 teaspoons vegetable or sunflower oil
¼ teaspoon cumin powder
¼ teaspoon coriander powder
¼ teaspoon turmeric powder
2 tablespoons fresh fenugreek leaves
  (or fresh coriander or another leaf of
  your choice), finely chopped
¼ teaspoon of salt

1. Mash the potatoes until smooth. These could be leftover potatoes!
2. Heat the oil in a large, non-stick frying pan over a medium-high heat.
3. Once the oil is hot, add the cumin powder, coriander powder and turmeric powder and mix them all in the oil for a minute.
4. Add the fresh fenugreek leaves, stirring to wilt them down slightly for 2–3 minutes.
5. Add the mashed potato and salt and mix well, heating through for another 2–3 minutes. Leave to cool.

Now turn to page 68.

Kottu Roti

You chose Colourful Mixed Vegetables, who can help you make Kottu Roti.

Mixed vegetables could be frozen vegetables or a mixture of any of your favourite fresh vegetables. Leftover vegetable curry is good too.

Traditionally, kottu roti is made with a flaky, layered flatbread called veechu or godamba roti. But any leftover flatbread can be used. 'Kottu' means 'chopped', which makes it not only tasty to eat but fun to watch being made, too. Street sellers in Sri Lanka clang their cleavers or sharp dough scrapers, each with their own unique rhythm, cutting up and mixing the rotis and curry on a hot plate. Who said food couldn't be musical?

Have a quick read of pages 19–21 before you try out this recipe.

2 servings
40 minutes

4 Roti Canai (page 37)
200ml cold water
1 teaspoon salt

For the vegetables
330g mixed vegetables or leftover curry
   (such as the samosa curry on page 36) or
   use the following ingredients:
2 tablespoons (30ml) ghee
45g onions, finely chopped
50g sweet peppers, finely chopped
90g cabbage, shredded
130g carrots, coarsely grated
60g peas
5-6 curry leaves, ripped
½ teaspoon cumin powder
½ teaspoon coriander powder
½ teaspoon chilli flakes or chilli powder

1. Chop the rotis into 1 x 2cm pieces.
2. If you're using leftover curry (one with lots of sauce works well), you simply need to warm it up in a frying pan. The curry and roti will have enough salt, but you may need to add a little water if the curry is too dry. If you're using frozen vegetables, simply cook them through for 5–10 minutes with sprinklings of water and salt.
3. But if you want to try something different, heat a large, non-stick frying pan over a medium-high heat and add 2 tablespoons of ghee.
4. Once the ghee has melted, add the onions and stir-fry them for 1–2 minutes, until soft and slightly brown.
5. Add the rest of the vegetables (peppers, carrots, cabbage, peas) and stir. Sprinkle over 4–5 tablespoons of water and cook the vegetables for 3–4 minutes.
6. Add the salt, curry leaves, cumin powder, coriander powder and chilli powder, and mix well. Add 4–5 more tablespoons of water.
7. Place a lid on the pan and reduce the heat to let the vegetables simmer and cook for 2–3 minutes.
8. Add the chopped roti and another 4–5 tablespoons of water and cook for another 2–3 minutes. Traditionally, kottu roti is quite dry, but adding water helps the roti pieces soften and absorb the spices, making it more delicious. (It is also tasty with more curry sauce.)
9. Serve while hot and enjoy!

Now turn to page 68.

Trofie

You chose Basil, who can help you make Trofie. Basil is a popular herb thanks to its sweet aroma and flavour. Go smell it and you'll immediately think of dishes you've eaten before. Our brains can link smells to memories!

Trofie are thin, twisty pasta pieces that are hand-rolled, and famous in the Liguria region of northern Italy. Which is also the same region that invented pesto, a dazzly basil-y paste!

Have a quick read of pages 19–21 before you try out this recipe.

Have a quick read of pages 19–21 before you try out this recipe.

4 servings
1 hour 30 minutes

200g plain, durum wheat or type '00' flour (popular in pasta-making)
100ml warm water, recently boiled
2 teaspoons salt
Cold water, for boiling
A drizzle of olive oil
2 tablespoons grated cheese of your choice
10–15 large fresh basil leaves, ripped up

1. In a bowl, mix the flour and warm water together with 1 teaspoon of salt until you have a dough.
2. Place the dough onto a smooth surface and knead it for 6–7 minutes.
3. Leave the dough to rest for 10 minutes, covering it with the bowl so it doesn't dry out.
4. Now to hand-roll the trofie. It takes a bit of practice, but it can be done! Take a small pea-sized piece of dough (1–2g) and place it on a smooth surface. Using your flat, open palm, roll the dough piece upwards to form a thin sausage shape. As you roll the piece back downwards, roll it diagonally as well, pressing slightly so that the joints of your fingers make dents in the pasta. This turns each shape into a swirl.
5. Repeat until you have enough pasta to eat. If each piece is exactly the same they'll cook equally. But the art of hand-rolling pasta takes practice, so don't worry if they all look different. (If easier, simply roll each small ball into a thin sausage shape, pinch the ends to make them pointy and twist in the middle.)
6. Pour some water into a large pan with a teaspoon of salt and bring to the boil.
7. Add your freshly made pasta to the pan, and once the trofie start to float (within 2–3 minutes), they're ready. Use a slotted spoon to scoop the pasta out of the water, or drain using a colander.
8. Once drained, add the pasta to a bowl, drizzle olive oil over the top and sprinkle the cheese and basil leaves on top (or try the bonus recipe on page 65 and add pesto). Mix well and serve!

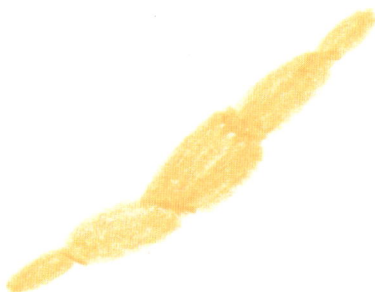

Basil Pesto

15 minutes

80g sunflower seeds, pine nuts or any
   seed or nut of your choice
40–50g fresh basil leaves
120–150ml olive oil
100g grated cheese of your choice
2–3g (1 small clove) garlic, finely
   chopped (optional)

1. If you're using sunflower seeds or pine nuts, toast these first in a dry pan over a medium heat for 2–3 minutes for extra flavour and to soften them.
2. Using a blender, or a pestle and mortar (or even the end of a rolling pin and a bowl as a DIY pestle and mortar), grind and crush the basil leaves and seeds or nuts together. Traditional pesto from Genoa uses garlic, so you can add this too, if you'd like. It'll take strong arms and about 10 minutes to make hand-made coarse pesto, but it's totally worth the effort.
3. Mix in the olive oil and cheese, then stir this into your pasta, and watch as the pesto coats all the trofie. (You don't have to use it all in one go. Keep any extra in a clean jar in the fridge for up to 1 week to use later.)

Now turn to page 68.

Pide

You chose Spinach, who can help you make Pide, pronounced 'pea-deh'. Spinach is a leafy green packed full of vitamins and minerals. It was mentioned in one of the oldest cookbooks from AD 1390, *The Forme of Cury*, as 'spinnedge'.

Pide is a bread base in the shape of a boat or canoe. It can be open or closed, and you can choose anything to fill it. Traditionally, pide is cooked in a brick or stone oven, which can cook breads faster because the bricks and stones get hotter than any modern-day oven, also trapping lots of steam for a tasty crust. In some regions of Turkey, pides are served at funerals in celebration of and to honour the loved one's life. In Georgia, a similar boat-shaped bread called khachapuri, with thicker crusts and a cheesy filling, has its own celebration day on 27 February!

Have a quick read of pages 19–21 before you try out this recipe.

4 servings
1 hour, and 1 hour resting time

450g strong white bread or plain flour, and a
    little extra for dusting
2 teaspoons instant dried yeast
1 teaspoon salt, and a little extra for the filling
290ml warm water
3 tablespoons garlic butter, melted
400g fresh spinach leaves
120g crumbled feta cheese, or any cheese of
    your choice (optional)

1. Add the flour to a bowl, then add the yeast to one side of the bowl and the salt to the opposite side. Make a well in the middle and add the warm water. Mix well until it becomes a dough.

2. Knead the dough in the bowl for about 10 minutes until smooth. If it's too sticky while kneading, add a little flour. Rub a teaspoon of melted garlic butter around the insides of the bowl, to stop the dough from sticking to the sides and to flavour it.

3. Leave the dough in the bowl for 1 hour, covered with a clean tea towel.

4. While waiting for the dough to prove, make the filling. In a large, non-stick frying pan over a medium heat, add 1 tablespoon of garlic butter and, if your butter is unsalted and you're not using cheese later, add a pinch of salt to taste.

5. Add the spinach leaves and stir for 4–5 minutes, or until it wilts and most of the water has evaporated. Turn off the heat and leave to cool for 5–10 minutes. Crumble in the feta cheese, if using, and mix everything together.

6. When the dough has doubled in size, knock or gently punch the dough, then split it in half.

7. Preheat the oven to 200°C (180°C fan). Line a large baking tray and dust with flour.

8. Roll out the two balls of dough into oval shapes, about 35 x 20cm and 5mm thick. Lay these on the baking tray.

9. Split the spinach filling into two and add to the middle of each oval, leaving a 2cm border around the edge. Fold these edges over like a crust to stop the filling from spilling. Squeeze the ends of each oval so they're pointy. Now each oval should look like a boat.

10. Bake the pides in the oven for 20–25 minutes. You'll know they're ready when the crusts are light golden brown.

11. Take the baking tray out of the oven and brush the rest of the melted garlic butter on the crusts.

12. Leave to cool slightly, cut into slices widthways and enjoy!

Now turn to page 68.

The End . . . or is it?

The more you read this book to find all 38 recipes and 47 ingredients*, the more you'll notice similarities and links between the riddles, the history, the science, the languages and the luscious dishes.

Food is a part of everyone's culture and daily lives, and all our favourite dishes tend to share common 'ancestors' – just like us as humans. The more we travel, the more we meet others and learn about different foods and cultures, borrowing ideas and trialling new combinations of ingredients, because we love to share deliciously comforting meals with our family and friends. The dishes may evolve, but at the same time we discover just how similar our foods – and we – are. There is so much more to food than the eating. Hopefully this book will inspire you to find out more about traditional recipes and the ways we have adapted these over the years.

I do hope you've enjoyed reading this book, working your way through the little foody adventures and having a go at the recipes, too! Why not pop back to page 3 to try another adventure? Or head straight to the Recipe Index (page 76) to cook up another treat.

*Did you find all the extra ingredient friends who joined in with the recipes? Some of them even appear on more than one occasion. And the recipes where water made a guest appearance?

Glossary

Absorb: to soak up.

Accompaniment: a food (or drink) that goes well with another food.

Airtight: used to describe a food container that won't let any air in, which means the water (and any bacteria or fungi) in the air can't reach the food. This stops the food spoiling. (See 'Spoil'.)

Bake: using dry heat from an oven to cook a dish.

Beat: stirring ingredients together really quickly.

Brine: a salt solution (salt dissolved in water).

Brush: using a pastry brush to cover a dough surface in melted butter, oil or milk.

Chop: to cut fruits and vegetables into small pieces or cubes.

Churn: the fast stirring, mixing and shaking of cream or milk to make butter.

Coarse: see 'Grate'.

Combine: mixing all ingredients thoroughly.

Consistency: the thickness or runnyness of a mixture. Dropping consistency means a mixture that drops smoothly off the spoon. Soft dropping consistency, such as for cake and pancake batters, is when the mixture slides off the spoon in a smooth stream when tipped, and stiff dropping consistency is when the mixture falls off the spoon when tipped but after a bit of a shake.

Core: removing the middle part, usually of a fruit, which contains the seeds.

Cream: beating ingredients such as sugar and butter to a smooth, light mixture.

Crystallise: when crystals form, such as in a rich sugar syrup, as it cools. The sucrose molecules join together, forming crystals. Lemon juice is an acid and breaks sucrose down into glucose and fructose, known as inversion, to stop the syrup crystallising. Crystallised ginger is either dried ginger rolled in sugar or ginger that has been cooked in sugar syrup and dried so the water evaporates, leaving the ginger coated in sugar crystals.

Curdle: when an acid is added to warmed milk making it thicken and separate into solid curds and liquid whey. Adding live yoghurt to almost boiled and cooled milk gives the milk a good bacteria (such as *Lactobacillus*) starter culture, which can turn the whole thing to yoghurt. This thickening is why yoghurt is also sometimes called curd. (See 'Fermentation'.)

Deep-fry: cooking food in a lot of oil, so that the food can float in the oil during cooking. (See 'Shallow-fry'.)

Density: how much stuff (mass) we have in a given space (volume). An ingredient that is less dense will be lighter and float on top of an ingredient that is more dense.

Diameter: measuring the straight line through the centre of a circle or sphere of dough.

Dissolve: when a solid such as salt or sugar is mixed with a liquid such as water to become a solution. Gases can also be dissolved in liquids.

Drain: to pour off the liquid, such as draining boiled water from cooked pasta, usually using a colander or sieve.

Drizzle: gently pouring a liquid, such as oil or runny icing, over the top of a dish.

Dropping consistency: see 'Consistency'.

Dry ingredients: see 'Well'.

Dust: lightly sprinkling powdery ingredients such as icing sugar or flour onto the surface or tops of foods. We dust surfaces when kneading dough, so it is less sticky and easier to work with.

Enriched dough: adding milk, butter, oil or cream to a dough, making it richer and pastry-like.

Evaporate: when a liquid turns into a gas, such as water turning to steam.

Extract: taking out an ingredient, such as a flavour, oil, spice or nut from the whole plant.

Fermentation: when microorganisms such as good bacteria (for example *Lactobacillus*) or yeast break down foods, releasing lactic acid (which helps in pickling) or carbon dioxide (which helps breads rise) or alcohol (when brewing).

Fermentation, like most reactions, speeds up in warm environments. We can also make non-fermented pickles, such as pickled onions, simply by soaking onions in a vinegary brine. We ferment and pickle vegetables to preserve them. This means they last longer, without the need for a fridge, and we can enjoy them during seasons when we can't grow them.

Fine: see 'Grate'.

Fold: combining light ingredients together slowly, without losing the air. It can also mean folding pastry into shapes, just as we fold paper.

Fry: see 'Deep-fry' or 'Shallow-fry'.

Gluten: a protein found in grains such as wheat and barley that makes dough stretchy. Gluten acts as a net, stretched around the carbon dioxide bubbles, helping the dough to rise during proving, which gives bread its spongy texture. (See 'Proving'.) Gluten-free flours, such as corn, rice or potato flour, are perfect for those who can't eat gluten, but the textures of food made with these flours can be very different to those containing gluten.

Golden brown: used to describe the colour of a well-baked or fried food.

Grate: creating coarse (large) or fine (small) shreds of cheese or vegetables. We also use the words 'coarse' and 'fine' to describe different-sized grains of sugar, and whether a paste such as pesto is smoothly ground or not.

Grease: coating the tray or baking dish with oil, butter or margarine so that food doesn't stick to it when baked in the oven, and to keep the greaseproof lining paper in place. (See 'Line'.)

Grind: when breaking up large food pieces into smaller ones, such as grain or dried peas into flour or olives into a paste, using a mill, food processor or pestle and mortar.

Inversion: see 'Crystallise'.

Knead: mixing dough with your hands or a mixer to make the dough strong, smooth and stretchy (elastic) by helping gluten to form. Kneading too much is known as overworking the dough. With scone and cookie doughs, overworking will give a bread-like chewiness. Overworking bread dough can damage the gluten and the dough won't stretch anymore.

Knock: also known as 'punching'. A way to pop most of the gas bubbles after the dough's first prove. This makes it easier to shape or mould the dough and gives the bread a fine, even texture. (See 'Prove'.)

Line: adding greaseproof paper to a baking tray or dish so that food doesn't stick to it when baked in the oven. Or adding kitchen roll to a plate to drain excess oil from fried foods. (See 'Grease'.)

Mash: to crush an ingredient, such as potatoes, until smooth, soft and almost creamy.

Minerals: such as calcium, sodium and potassium, are found on Earth and in our foods to help our bodies work normally. Vitamins such as vitamin A and C are also needed for good health – for growing, healing wounds and boosting our immune system. Eating a variety of foods can help us get all the minerals and vitamins (or micronutrients) we need.

Moderation: 'everything in moderation' means we can enjoy a variety of dishes, cooked in different ways, but not overdo it. Too much sugar, salt and fat is not good for our health.

Overwork: see 'Knead'.

Peel: removing the skin from a fruit or vegetable, or the name of the skin itself, such as lemon peel.

Pickle: see 'Fermentation'.

Pinch: a small amount, usually measured by picking up an ingredient such as salt between your thumb and forefinger. About an eighth of a teaspoon.

Preheat: heating up the oven to the correct temperature before putting bakes in. This is important for cakes and breads that need to be cooked at a high heat straight away to get them to rise well.

Preserve: a method of keeping food so it doesn't spoil, and stays safe. This includes pickling, fermenting, canning, freezing, or even cooking fruit whole in sugar, which is why some jams and marmalades are known as 'preserves'.

Prove: also known as 'proof', is when bread dough is left to rise. Yeast breaks down the starch in the flour, producing carbon dioxide gas. The bubbles of gas stretch the gluten net, and the dough expands like a balloon. The first prove takes about an hour, and the dough will double in size. The dough is then knocked, shaped and left to prove a second time. This helps the yeast work a little more, giving the bread a better texture and flavour. (See 'Fermentation', 'Gluten' and 'Knock'.)

Punch: see 'Knock'.

Raising agents: such as baking powder (found in self-raising flour) and bicarbonate of soda. These are used to make cakes and breads light and fluffy. Raising agents work because an acid and alkali react together to release carbon dioxide, and these bubbles of gas make batters light. If the batter contains heavy ingredients, such as dried fruit or shredded vegetables, more than one raising agent may be needed. Self-raising flour also creates crumblier crumble toppings and cookies.

Rest: leaving any dough for a while before shaping or kneading. The starch and gluten in the dough absorb water and relax, making it easier to work with.

Rub: using your fingertips and thumbs to squish the fat into the flour so that small grains of flour stick together with small bits of fat, creating breadcrumb-like pieces.

Savoury: how we describe foods that are not sweet, and usually salty or spicy.

Shallow-fry: cooking food in a small amount of oil, about 1cm or so in depth in the frying pan. The food will be at the bottom of the pan during cooking. Adding enough oil to coat the pan is known as 'pan-frying'. (See 'Deep-fry'.)

Shred: chopping an ingredient finely, either with a sharp knife or food processor (see 'Grate').

Sift: shaking flour or icing sugar through a sieve, to remove large lumps, making all the particles equal, and to add more air for a lighter texture.

Simmer: heating a pan of water or ingredients until it is about to boil, then reducing the heat so it keeps bubbling gently.

Spoil: when food goes off or bad, usually because bacteria or fungi start to break down the food and it's no longer safe to eat. When there is hardly any water in a food (such as powdered milk or crackers), it makes it more difficult for bacteria or fungi to grow, so the food doesn't spoil easily. Storing foods at lower temperatures (such as in the fridge or freezer) can slow down the spoiling process too, especially in foods containing water.

Starch: a large carbohydrate made up of lots of glucose molecules. Flour and potatoes contain a lot of starch. Some potatoes are known as floury potatoes because they are high in starch but low in water, and others are known as waxy potatoes because they are low in starch and high in water.

Steam: the gas form of water. Steaming foods means using a steamer, colander or rack over simmering hot water, to cook a dish with moist heat. Cooked gnocchi float because the tiny air pockets in the dough heat up and expand,

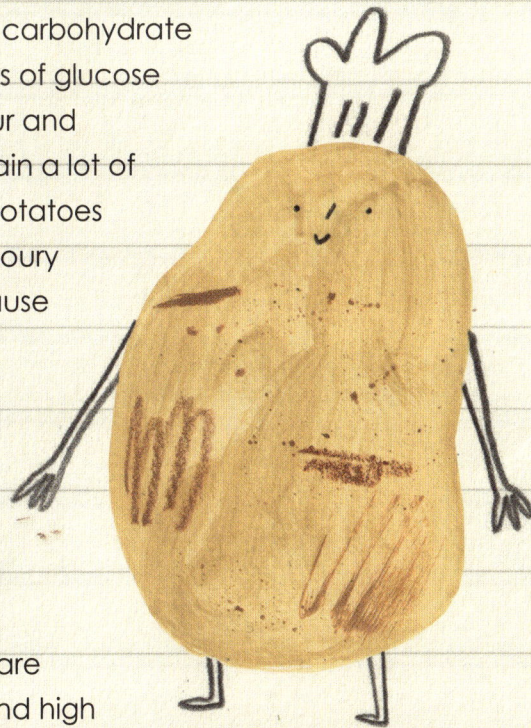

but the water inside each gnocco also turns to steam. The gnocchi are then less dense than the surrounding water, so they float. At the same time, the expanding hot air and steam cook the dough from the inside, so the gnocchi taste perfectly pillowy and soft.

To taste: when adding salt, pepper, sugar or spices to your own liking, so there's no exact measurement.

Toast: moving seeds or nuts around in a hot dry pan for a few minutes, allowing them to release their own oils, slowly becoming warm, golden brown and toasty.

Vitamins: see 'Minerals'.

Wedge: a piece of fruit or cheese that has a triangular shape, such as a citrus fruit segment, usually with its skin on.

Well: making a dip in the dry ingredients (such as flour, baking powder and sugar mixed together), which makes it easier to pour in the wet ingredients (such as water, milk and oil) and combine them gradually using a circular movement, into a smooth batter with no lumps.

Wet ingredients: see 'Well'.

Whisk: using a fork, hand whisk or electric whisk to beat the ingredients together, adding in lots of air to make a light batter or mixture.

Wilt: heating up leafy greens in a pan so the water comes out of the leaves, and they cook in this water. Plants in the garden or in pots can also wilt from a lack of water.

The Recipes

Kitchen Creations Nigel Lawson

Speedy Sauces

DELISH RECIPES Lucia Vinti

The Recipe Index

YEAST

Notes

Acknowledgements

Firstly I'd like to thank the wonderful Leah Thaxton, Natasha Brown, Rachel Malig and all at Faber Children's for taking on my foody adventure and helping me turn it into the deliciously luscious thing that it is now. Lucia Vinti's gorgeous illustrations, Suzanne Stougie's expert eye for recipes and Matthew McFall's wondrous gamebook knowledge have all been the icing on the cake!

Many thanks are due of course to my lovely family and friends, who are always willing volunteers to eat everything I bake, and especially to my amazing mum, who taught me that there's so much more to recipes and still allows me to be her sous chef after all these years . . . even if I'm just chatting away in her kitchen!

Finally, just as a main dish is nothing without accompaniments, thank you to all the following fabulous people (and many of their contacts) for feedback, advice, support and general merriment. Apologies for making you all hungry while reading drafts, but you're all amazing and I truly appreciate everything you've done.

Philip Ahn, Zahra Alhumaidi, Michelle Anderson, Masaō Ashtine, Rita Barone, British Mexican Society, Sara Canullo, Lesley Chamberlain, Josh Chamot, Jeevani Charika, Sunita Chawdhary, Cirilo Filipino Kainan Restaurant, Tom Cook, Ersin Coskun, Paul Couchman, Emily Dawson, Françoise Dawson, Rohini Deshmukh, Penny Fletcher, Michele Gemelos, Alex Goldsmith, Kathryn Harkup, High Timber Restaurant, Jeanne Horak, Martin Hurajt, Naomi Huzovicova, Japan Centre, Prem Kumar, Perina Lobendahn, Richard Lowkes, Rachel Lucero – The Sago Show, Elena Mallickova, Jane Malyon, Roisin Markham, Ada Mau, Dominic McDonald, Rehana Mughal, Allan Njanji, Rahul Patel, Amelie Persson, Pircio Restaurant, Louise Roberts – Alimenti Food Sciences, Pia Schreiber, Alom Shaha, Ellie Smith, Louie Stowell, Andrew Taylor, Miki Tomita, Gyorgy Turan, Julia Turan, Colin Volavola, Liv Wan and Bekele Woyecha.

First published in 2023
by Faber & Faber Limited
Bloomsbury House,
74–77 Great Russell Street,
London WC1B 3DA
faber.co.uk

Typeset in Century Gothic by Friederike Huber
Printed in India

A CIP record for this book is available from the British Library

ISBN 978–0–571–37064–1

MIX
Paper from responsible sources
FSC
www.fsc.org
FSC® C016779

Printed and bound on FSC paper in line with our continuing commitment to ethical business practices, sustainability and the environment.
For further information see faber.co.uk/environmental-policy

2 4 6 8 10 9 7 5 3 1